Everybody loves
MORBID CURIOSITY

"Alan has written a very funny, very clever book—it's shocking and sinful, and I couldn't put it down. He leaves no gravestone unturned, nothing buried. *Morbid Curiosity* is part *Six Feet Under*, part *Mad* magazine. It'll make a killing!"

—Joan Rivers

"Even celebrities eventually die. In fact they do so in far more rivetingly grand-scale ways than mere mortals. And now that they've met their maker, they've also found their chronicler. Alan W. Petrucelli unearths the demises of the rich and famous—from Valentino to Heath Ledger and beyond—with detailed research, dishy wit, and insight. This book is to die for!"

—Michael Musto

"*Morbid Curiosity* is a cornucopia of Hollywood gossip and tidbits, much more humorous than macabre, delivered from a different point of view than any book I've read about celebs. Who knew Al Jolson died in the same hotel suite in San Francisco in which Fatty Arbuckle's career was ruined? Who knew Merv Griffin's tombstone reads, 'I will not be right back after this message'? It's breezy, pithy, informative, odd, and, despite its subject matter, certain to amuse."

—Robert Osborne, host of *Turner Classic Movies*

"I couldn't put the book down until I finished reading every word. Isn't it interesting how people are fascinated with the subject of death . . . especially when you get older? As someone once said, 'The first thing I read is the obit page to see if my name's there!' You couldn't have picked a better title. It's a terrific read for those who have to know every little detail about the famous and infamous. Some great stories to be told at the dinner table. Can't wait to give my next dinner party!"

—Rona Barrett

MORBID CURIOSITY

The Disturbing Demises of the Famous and Infamous

ALAN W. PETRUCELLI

A PERIGEE BOOK

A PERIGEE BOOK
Published by the Penguin Group
Penguin Group (USA) Inc.
375 Hudson Street, New York, New York 10014, USA
Penguin Group (Canada), 90 Eglinton Avenue East, Suite 700, Toronto, Ontario M4P
2Y3, Canada (a division of Pearson Penguin Canada Inc.)
Penguin Books Ltd., 80 Strand, London WC2R 0RL, England
Penguin Group Ireland, 25 St. Stephen's Green, Dublin 2, Ireland (a division of
Penguin Books Ltd.)
Penguin Group (Australia), 250 Camberwell Road, Camberwell, Victoria 3124,
Australia (a division of Pearson Australia Group Pty. Ltd.)
Penguin Books India Pvt. Ltd., 11 Community Centre, Panchsheel Park, New Delhi—
110 017, India
Penguin Group (NZ), 67 Apollo Drive, Rosedale, North Shore 0632, New Zealand
(a division of Pearson New Zealand Ltd.)
Penguin Books (South Africa) (Pty.) Ltd., 24 Sturdee Avenue, Rosebank, Johannesburg
2196, South Africa

Penguin Books Ltd., Registered Offices: 80 Strand, London WC2R 0RL, England

While the author has made every effort to provide accurate telephone numbers and
Internet addresses at the time of publication, neither the publisher nor the author
assumes any responsibility for errors, or for changes that occur after publication.
Further, the publisher does not have any control over and does not assume any
responsibility for author or third-party websites or their content.

First edition: October 2009

Library of Congress Cataloging-in-Publication Data

Petrucelli, Alan W., 1958–
   Morbid curiosity : the disturbing demises of the famous and infamous /
Alan W. Petrucelli.— 1st ed.
      p.   cm.
   Includes bibliographical references and index.
   ISBN 978-0-399-53527-7
   1. Celebrities—Death—Miscellanea.   I. Title.
   CT105.P483 2009
   306.9—dc22   2009022409

PRINTED IN THE UNITED STATES OF AMERICA

10   9   8   7   6   5   4   3   2

Most Perigee books are available at special quantity discounts for bulk purchases for
sales promotions, premiums, fund-raising, or educational use. Special books, or book
excerpts, can also be created to fit specific needs. For details, write: Special Markets,
Penguin Group (USA) Inc., 375 Hudson Street, New York, New York 10014.

For Stephen J. Finn,
who introduced me to a world inhabited by Cuddles Bardwell,
Eric Cartman, Eva Le Gallienne, Marsha Hunt, Russ Meyer,
Barbara Nichols, Barbara Payton, Ann Savage, Tura Satana,
Claire Trevor, Edgar G. Ulmer,
曾詠韓, William Winter, Cornell Woolrich,
hirsute hydrocephalic midgets, and other memorable characters.
Every time I have fallen he has picked me up.
Every time I have embraced darkness, he has shown me the light.
I doubt there is a kinder, gentler, more loving man.

CONTENTS

INTRODUCTION

I've laughed with Lucy (1911–1989), cried with Karloff (1887–1969), kibitzed with Kafka (1883–1924), meditated with Garbo (1905–1990), booed at Billy the Kid (1859–1881), chatted with Crawford (Joan, 1905–1977, and Broderick, 1911–1986), even planted New Guinea impatiens at the grave of Linda Darnell (1923–1965)—and you thought she was pushing up daisies.

I've held urns with the cremains of Ferdinando Nicola Sacco (1891–1927), Bartolomeo Vanzetti (1888–1927), and Judy Tyler (1933–1957) in my hands; jumped over a locked gate protecting the privacy of Jean Harlow (1911–1937) (yes, I was caught and reprimanded); and attended the standing-room-only funeral of Jane Wyman (1917–2007), who was laid to rest in a plain coffin and dressed in a nun's habit since she was a member of the Dominican Order of the Catholic Church.

I've prayed at the tombstones of everyone from A (Abbott, Bud, 1895–1974) to Z (Zimbalist, Efrem Sr., 1890–1985).

I've even . . . I'll give it a rest and leave some things buried.

Such grave matters, this thing I have for dead celebs.

And I know what you're dying to ask: Why?

Blame Basil.

As a child, I paid weekly visits to the grave of my grandmother, interred in a crypt in the Shrine of Memories at Ferncliff, a cemetery and mausoleum in Westchester County, New York. I was eleven, maybe twelve, and remember an aunt telling me that "Sherlock Holmes" was buried in the same building.

Sherlock Holmes? She must mean the definitive film Sherlock, Basil Rathbone (1892–1967)! Even back then, while classmates were discussing sports and the joys of the opposite sex, I was watching *The Late Show*, wishing I could dance like Fred (or Ginger), convincing worried family members that the fruit plate on my head was actually an emergency ration of vitamins B, C, and D—and sleuthing with the best private dick of them all.

Once I discovered Basil's grave (Unit 1, Tier K, Crypt 117), dead celebs took their resting spots in my brain alongside old movies and trivial trivia, and I knew I didn't have a prayer of stopping. I began clipping obituaries. I plunged into research. (Imagine my delight when I found out my paternal grandmother's grave was across from Eddie Foy, 1856–1928, and his famous vaudevillian family of seven little Foys at Holy Sepulchre Cemetery in New Rochelle, New York.)

Even back then, before I began getting paid for telling all about celebrities, I was digging the dirt. One Ferncliff salesman told me that Rathbone walked in one day to make final arrangements for him and his wife, Ouida (1885–1974). "I don't believe in spending lots of money," he told the salesman, "especially when I am dead." And so Rathbone chose the least expensive spot. Ferncliff's crypts are aligned in vertical rows; those at eye level are the most expensive, the cheapest are *waaaay* up touching the ceiling. Rathbone and wife chose two cheap seats. Each week, I'd strain my neck and pay my respects to Basil and Ouida. One day I noticed that Cornell Woolrich (1903–1968) was buried a few yards from Rathbone. His was an expensive, eye-level grave. Woolrich may be a footnote in most celeb circles, but to mystery and noir fans, he's a literary giant, considered a genius of the crime genre. The man who wrote *Rear Window*! Gay! Dead! And buried next to his mother, whom he never allowed to read his work. How much better does it get?

Much better. As I continued the unearthing, Ferncliff became my new playground. The "Forest Lawn of the East" was the final home to such notables as Joan Crawford (1905–1977), Judy Garland (1922–1969), Thelonious Monk (1917–1982), Moms Mabley (1884–1975), Malcolm X (1925–1965), Harold Arlen (1905–1986), Ed Sullivan (1901–1974), Diana Sands (1934–1973), Tom Carvel (1906–1990), Paul Robeson (1898–1976), James Baldwin (1924–1987), and Jerome Kern (1845–1945). The list is as long as a really good eulogy for a really liked person. In recent years, Aaliyah (1979–2001) and Kitty Carlisle Hart (1910–2007), who was reunited with her hubby, Moss Hart (1904–1961), have joined the permanent, hermetically sealed ranks. (The fact that Kitty went back to Moss was a bit curious since she told me she was going to be buried at her family's plot in New Orleans.)

Even those not staying a lifetime pay visits to Ferncliff: John Lennon (1940–1980), Jim Henson (1936–1990), and Nelson Rockefeller (1908–1979) were cremated here; in 1988, the remains of Bela Bartok (1881–1945) were disinterred and sent back to his native Hungary.

And so my obsession grew. And grew. And grew. As I grew older and began my writing career, I traveled around the world, to this country's and that one's graveyards, taking notes and photos, and always leaving behind prayers and thoughts . . . sometimes a rock if I was in the Jewish part of town.

Once I began working for national magazines—my first professional story was the obit of actor David Janssen (1931–1980) that ran in *Photoplay*—I'd ask my subjects questions about death and dying, and everyone had a story.

Lucille Ball (1911–1989) complained that all the awards and accolades she got during her lifetime made her feel dead; years later, Lucy's daughter Lucie Arnaz remembered the morning that the crypt of her mother was being sealed and how guilty she felt because she could not cry.

Bette Midler and Cher wept when they recalled how many friends they had lost to AIDS.

Richard Carpenter lashed out at Joan Rivers's "sick" jokes about the anorexia that eventually killed his sister Karen Carpenter (1950–1983).

Liza Minnelli and Lorna Luft admitted that they never visit the grave of their mom, Judy Garland, nor have they ever sent flowers. Liza said, "That grave is not my mother. Mama remains alive. She always will be. Why should I stand in front of something that's not really her?" Lorna added, "Judy Garland lives on in films and music and TV. She has never died. Her legacy is what counts, not some gravestone with her name on it."

Anthony Newley (1931–1999) told me he so hated his former wife Joan Collins that he couldn't wait until she was dead, calling her "a commodity who would sell her own bowel movement."

Carly Simon tearfully remembered how she "lost a good friend" when her Martha's Vineyard neighbor, Jackie Onassis, died of cancer of the lymphatic system.

My interview with Anne Baxter (1923–1985) became her obituary—two days after we chatted in her California home, she flew to New York and while walking down Madison Avenue, suffered a brain aneurysm and died, with passersby ignoring her body thinking she was a well-dressed bag lady. (One man finally summoned an ambulance and she was rushed to Lenox Hill Hospital, where she died.) Mine was the last interview Anne would ever give. One of the more memorable quotes: "People can call me a legend when I'm dead."

Suzanne Somers, who was diagnosed with breast cancer in 2001, told me she is certain her decision to refuse chemotherapy, opting instead to take hormones and homeopathic treatments, continues to keep her alive. "My husband is Jewish and he says, 'dead is dead,' but I do believe we've been here before and we'll be here again."

When I told Dennis Hopper that actress Betsy Palmer told me she was the "only woman" James Dean ever slept with before his death, he howled, long and loudly, gasping for breath, until finally asking, "What $%&#$%! drugs was she on?"

Dolly Parton's final wish? "I'm not ready to go yet, but when I do get to those pearly gates, I want God to pat me on the head and say, 'You did good!' I want to be remembered as someone who touched people and left behind worthwhile things for them to enjoy. I want to be remembered for being a good person who had a lot of love to give."

Reba McEntire's preferred epitaph? "Mom really did some good on this earth."

I will never tell the best dish I was ever served—a once-famous actor told me not to believe what I had heard about the death of "Mama" Cass Elliot (1941–1974) . . . then proceeded to regale me with details of how she "really" died. I'll save that one for another day. Or book.

In 1981 I received, in a rather academic yet amusing way, "validation" about my passed-on pastime. I had flown to California to interview Swiss-born psychiatrist Elisabeth Kübler-Ross (1926–2004) for an *Us Weekly* feature. It took many weeks to secure the interview, but she had a new book to plug and I wanted to one day be able to brag that I got to sit "thisclose" to the world's leading authority on death and dying. We gabbed for hours, sitting across from each other in the living room of her comfy home, and I was delighted by Elisabeth's dry, almost wry, sense of humor. She understood that her theories and beliefs in re-incarnation and "afterlife entities" had made her the target of much ribbing, but she also understood that her ground-breaking 1969 work *On Death and Dying* would not die—oops! make its "transition"—when she made hers.

Soon after the interview was published, I received a letter from Elisabeth's assistant informing me, in a single-spaced typed letter, that Kübler-Ross was angry because the title of the interview was "Doctor Death," a phrase she found "offensive." (The fact that the title came from my editor meant nothing.) I was deeply disappointed. I had always given Kübler-Ross credit when it came to my healthy obses-sion with death, and it was she who would give me, all those many years ago, the title for this tome.

"People don't die," she told me that afternoon. "They shed their bodies and transition. I don't really understand why Americans have such a morbid curiosity about death."

A series of strokes partially paralyzed her, yet Kübler-Ross's humor was still razor-sharp; in 2002, she quipped, "I told God last night that he's a damned procrastinator."

He stopped procrastinating two years later. Kübler-Ross's gravestone can be found in Paradise Memorial Gardens in Scottsdale, Arizona, where one and all are reminded that Doctor Death went on to "dance in the galaxies" on Au-gust 24, 2004.

Thanks, Elisabeth. And save a dance for me.

Lights! Action! Coffin!

HOLLYWOOD'S UNHAPPY FINAL ENDINGS, 1910–1970

Mass Hysteria

AH, star power. When Rudolph Valentino died (1895–1926) quite unexpectedly at age thirty-one of peritonitis, the world's great lover (who was bisexual) still managed to draw crowds. More than one hundred thousand mourners stood in line for hours to get a peek at his embalmed corpse resting so comfortably in the Gold Room of the Frank E. Campbell funeral home in New York City. Crowds were so eager to see their hero that floral wreaths were trampled and windows smashed; more than one hundred people were injured in the melee. One twenty-year-old fan was so distraught she killed herself; her suicide note read, "With his death, the last bit of courage has flown."

At the Los Angeles memorial service, movie star Pola Negri—who claimed she and Rudy were going to marry—showed up wearing a special gown she had designed at a cost of $3,000. Rudy is buried wearing a "slave bracelet" given to him by his estranged wife, Natacha Rambova. He was interred in a temporary crypt owned by June Mathis, the woman who discovered him. But when plans for a grand mausoleum never materialized, Rudy stayed on in Crypt 1205. When Mathis died in 1927, she was buried to the left of Valentino.

Blond Time Bomb

PLATINUM screen beauty Jean Harlow (1911–1937) was the screen's Blond Bombshell, but her inner bomb went off way too early. She died of uremic poisoning at twenty-six, and was buried in the flower-festooned pink gown she wore in her film *Libeled Lady*. The film costarred her lover, William Powell, who not only covered Jean's bronze casket with fifteen hundred lilies of the valley and five hundred gardenias, but paid $25,000 for a private imported-marble crypt at Forest Lawn. The inscription on her double-width tomb reminds one and all that Harlow remains OUR BABY. In her hand, she carries a white gardenia and unsigned note reading "Good night, my dearest darling." One guess who left those.

Final Fields Day

W. C. FIELDS (1880–1946) spent the last fourteen months of his life at Las Encinas Sanatorium in Pasadena, California, where friends would find him reading the Bible ("I'm checking for loopholes"). As he lay dying, his longtime lover Carlotta Monti would venture outside and turn the hose onto the roof so Fields could hear his favorite sound, falling rain. Fields died from a stomach hemorrhage on Christmas Day, a holiday he claimed to have hated. He smiled and winked at a nurse, put a finger to his lips, closed his eyes, and died as blood bubbled from his mouth. Fields was cremated and his ashes interred in the Forest Lawn Memorial Park Cemetery, in Glendale, California. No, his grave marker does not read "On the whole, I would rather be in Philadelphia" nor does it say "I'd rather be in Philadelphia"—variations of the oft-told urban legend.

The Big Sleep

THEY didn't have sleep number beds back then, so French actress Sarah Bernhardt (1844–1923) was forced to sleep in a rosewood coffin. It was during her early career that she acquired her coffin, claiming sleeping in it helped her understand her many tragic roles. The actress was always a step ahead of her time, having been one of the first women to play the title role of *Hamlet*. Even a decade-old injury (jumping off the parapet in the last scene of a production of *La Tosca*) that forced the amputation of her right leg in 1915 didn't keep her from returning to the stage using a fake leg. Sarah died of uremia in the arms of her son Maurice, and is buried in Paris's Cimetière du Père Lachaise, a gravestone decorated with a coffin marking the spot.

The Skinny on Fatty

WE have reservations about staying in Suite 1221 of the Westin St. Francis Hotel in San Francisco. That's the room in which the screams of starlet Virginia Rappe (1891–1921) led to the demise of comedian Roscoe "Fatty" Arbuckle's career. Rappe was one of the guests at Arbuckle's "wild" Labor Day weekend party. She fell sick during the festivities and died a few days later. Newspapers smelled a "scent"sational booze- and drug-filled sex murder and had a field day . . . but most of what was printed was speculation or lies. Fatty was accused of jumping on top of Rappe, causing her bladder to burst; raping her with a broken

Coke bottle, a champagne bottle, a sharp piece of ice (or all three); or crushing her with his massive 340-pound frame. The official cause of death? The former model with the reputation of dirty snow died from peritonitis from a burst bladder, the result of a botched abortion a week or so earlier. Two days after the scandal began, voluntary and state-mandated bans were imposed on Arbuckle's films; after three trials, the first two ending in hung juries, Arbuckle was finally acquitted in March 1922. But his career was over.

Nearly thirty years later, in the same hotel suite, Al Jolson (1886–1950) was just finishing a game of gin rummy when he fell to the floor, dying of a massive heart attack. Jolson's last words were "Boys, I'm going . . ."

To see Fatty?

Final Descents

HOLLYWOOD'S greatest screwball comedienne was also a great saleslady. Carole Lombard (1908–1942) had just sold $2,017,531 in war bonds, and told the Indianapolis crowds greeting her, "Before I say goodbye to you all, come on! Join me in a big cheer: V for victory!" She then flipped a coin to determine the best way to get back to Hollywood and her husband, Clark Gable. Train (she called it the "choo-choo") or plane? At 4 a.m., Carole, along with her mother and publicist, piled into a TWA twin engine DC-3 at the Indianapolis Airport. "When I get home," Lombard told a *Life* photographer at the airport, "I'll flop in bed and sleep for twelve hours."

After refueling in Las Vegas, the plane took off at 7:07 p.m., flying at an altitude of 8,100 feet and 13 degrees off-course. Twenty-three minutes later, the plane smashed into Table Rock Mountain, thirty miles southwest of Las Vegas. All twenty-two passengers were instantly killed, including fifteen military personnel. Two days later, Carole's charred remains were pulled from the snowy wreckage site; her body was found in the front section of the fuselage and she was identified by "a wisp of unscorched blond hair."

The army offered a military funeral to honor the first star to give her life to the war effort, but Gable refused and carried out Carole's wishes for a swift interment. What remained of Lombard (and by all account it was little; the unsigned tuft of hair, and remnants of the black gloves and strapless evening gown she had been wearing) was buried in a special white gown made by designer Irene and, in accordance with her will, was interred in a "modestly priced crypt" at Forest Lawn. When he died in 1960, Gable was laid to rest next to Lombard, though he had remarried twice. This was a move Gable's then-wife, Kay, insisted upon. When asked by a reporter where Gable would be buried, she simply said, "With Carole, of course. She was his greatest love."

ACTOR and author William "Will" Rogers (1879–1935) never met a man he didn't like. Not even Wiley Post. Rogers and the one-eyed aviator were on an around-the-world tour when their small plane crashed in a lagoon near Barrow, Alaska Territory, on August 15. Rogers, the highest-paid movie star at the time and a prolific writer whose work was syndicated in some four thousand newspapers, had been working on a column: When his mangled typewriter was extracted from the wreckage, the last word he had typed was "death."

A Blaze of Glory

SOMETIMES fame is so fleeting it can go up in smoke without any notice. Just ask Martha Mansfield (1899–1923) when you finally meet her in the Great Cinema in the Sky.

She was starting to make quite the name for herself until her career ended on November 29. She was filming *The Warrens of Virginia*, a big-budget Civil War melodrama in which she played the fiancée of a Confederate soldier; during a break, an assistant lit a cigarette, carelessly flicking the match in her direction. Faster than you could say, "Scarlett O'Hara," Mansfield's period costume went up in flames . . . and the actress with it. Crew and cast members feverishly tried to extinguish the fire, and the actress was rushed to the hospital with severe burns. She died at noon the following day.

THE woman regarded by many as the most beautiful actress who ever lived—her best friend Ann Miller gloated about her gorgeousness until the day she died—helped give new meaning to the phrase "ashes to ashes . . ." By the early 1960s Linda Darnell (1923–1965), was reduced to playing stock theater roles and spending her days and nights stuffing her face and drinking booze. While staying at the Glenview, Illinois, home of her former secretary Jeanne Curtis, the actress learned that one of her films, the 1940 flick *Star Dust*, was on TV. "Let's have some laughs," Darnell said.

So she, Jeanne, and Jeanne's sixteen-year-old daughter Patricia watched the film, going to bed at 2:20 in the morning. An hour later, a cigarette Darnell had been smoking, which was still smoldering, burst into flames. All three women got out in time, but Darnell ran back into the house, thinking Patricia was still inside. Wrong move—the girl had safely escaped. Darnell suffered burns over 80 percent of her body; fragments of her pajamas had fused to her flesh. Doctors worked on her for four hours and a tracheotomy was performed to help her breathe.

Despite Darnell's exclamations—"Who says I'm going to die? I'm not going to!"—she lived less than one day, eventually dying at 3:25 p.m. of a massive staph infection.

She was forty-one. She was cremated (naturally) and her ashes remained in storage for a decade before they were interred at Union Hill Cemetery in Kennett Square, Pennsylvania.

||||||||||||||||||||||||||||||||||||||||||||||||||||||||||||||||||||||||||||||||||||||||||||||||||||||||||||

Norman Spencer Chaplin (1919), the infant son of comic legend Charlie Chaplin, was nothing to laugh about. The baby's mother was sixteen-year-old child star Mildred Harris. Norman suffered from deforming birth defects and died after three days. The kid is buried in Inglewood Park Cemetery in Los Angeles, in a grave whose tombstone simply reads THE LITTLE MOUSE.   ☠

||||||||||||||||||||||||||||||||||||||||||||||||||||||||||||||||||||||||||||||||||||||||||||||||||||||||||||

Pulling a Boner

LONG before there was Zsa Zsa and Eva there was Lya De Putti (1899–1931), a Hungarian sexpot who first found fame in Germany. It wasn't long before Hollywood imported the black-haired pixie with the heart-shaped lips, hailing her as "the loveliest girl in Berlin." D. W. Griffith directed her American film debut in the 1926 silent hit *The Sorrows of Satan*, but it was the film for which she was first brought to this country (*Variety*) that remains the essential De Putti. But just as things were getting hot, fate dished out a variety of mishaps. And it all began with a chicken bone.

De Putti was living at the Hotel Buckingham in New York City when she realized something didn't feel right. Her throat was scratchy. She was having difficulty breathing. She was taken to a hospital; an X-ray revealed she had a chicken bone from a recent meal lodged in her throat. Doctors removed the bone, but De Putti's condition worsened. Days after the first operation, a second one was performed after doctors discovered a severe infection had set in. At first, there was hope: The actress seemed to be getting better, but pleurisy developed, followed by pneumonia. For days, the beauty was administered oxygen constantly. Lya De Putti expired at twenty-three, an age obviously more tender than the chicken she had savored less than two weeks earlier.

Road Rage

IT'S easy, perhaps too easy, to say that Jayne Mansfield (1933–1967) was eager to get ahead in life, especially since it has been widely believed that she was decapitated in the car crash that took her life at about 2:25 a.m. on June 29 on U.S. Highway 90, between Slidell and New Orleans, Louisiana.

Only the most ghoulish of death hounds and grave robbers would hope such a legend was true. The poor man's Monroe did suffer head trauma in the horrific accident. She was returning from a nightclub engagement when, as the driver rounded a curve on a dark stretch of highway, the gray 1966 Buick Electra 225 belonging to her then beau Sam Brody crashed into the rear of a tractor trailer that had slowed down because of a truck spraying for mosquitoes. The rumors of her decapitation started when crime photographs of the crashed car showed tufts of blond hair tangled in the smashed windshield. (It was either a wig that Mansfield was wearing or was her actual hair and scalp.) Her death certificate assures us that the immediate cause of Jayne's death was a "crushed skull with avulsion of cranium and brain." In other words, she was scalped. Brody was also instantly killed. Jayne's three children, Miklós, Zoltán, and Mariska (all by her ex-husband, bodybuilder and Mr. Universe Miklós "Mickey" Hargitay, who raised the kids with new wife Ellen Siano), were in the backseat and escaped with minor injuries. Mariska, the Emmy-winning star of *Law & Order: Special Victims Unit*, was three at the time and today bears a three-inch scar on one side of her face.

Following Jayne's death, the National Highway Traffic Safety Administration began mandating that an underride guard, a strong steel bar, be installed on all tractor trailers. This bar is known as a Mansfield bar.

SOME people would think Isadora Duncan (1877–1927) "auto" know better, especially since automobiles steered her to such nightmares. The woman known as the "Mother of Modern Dance" became a heavy drinker after the tragic deaths of her son and daughter on April 19, 1913; the children and their nanny were out for a ride when the car stalled on a hill overlooking the Seine River. The driver forgot to set the parking brake and, as he stepped out to inspect the engine, the vehicle rolled down the hill and sank into the water. Years later on the night of September 14, Duncan, wearing a long, draping silk scarf, went for a ride along France's Riviera. The driver had no idea that Duncan, sitting in the backseat of the convertible, was being strangled—her fringed scarf had become tangled around the open-spoke wheel and rear axle of the back tire. As the car took off so did Duncan, her body pulled and dragged several yards by the vehicle along the cobblestone street.

Duncan was cremated and her ashes were placed next to those of her beloved children in a columbarium at Père Lachaise Cemetery in Paris. Since Duncan was married to (but estranged from) Russian poet Sergei Yesenin, she was legally a Soviet citizen—Duncan's will was the first of a Soviet citizen probated in the United States. A bloody good afterthought: Ysenin hanged himself in the bathroom two years prior to Duncan's death; his suicide note was his final poem written in his blood, drawn from the wrists he had slit. The first two lines read: "Goodbye, my friend, good-bye / My love, you are in my heart."

WHATEVER happened to a simple game of cowboys and Indians? Western star Tom Mix (1880–1940) was killed in a less than dignified way. On October 12, as he was speeding in his 1937 Cord Sportsman through the Arizona desert on U.S. Highway 80, he came across some unexpected construction. Crews watched as he swerved and braked; the car plunged into a ravine. The sudden motions dislocated a large aluminum suitcase he had put on the seat behind him. It flew forward and struck Mix in the back of the head, shattering his skull and breaking his neck. The sixty-year-old Mix was nixed instantly. Police found $6,000 in cash and $1,500 in checks in his pockets. Mix is buried in Forest Lawn in Glendale, California, wearing white riding britches, handmade boots, and his trademark platinum belt buckle with his initials set in diamonds.

THE climax of the life of Friedrich Wilhelm Murnau (1888–1931), one of the most influential German film directors of the silent era and a pioneer in the expressionist movement, came on March 11 when he died in an automobile accident in Santa Barbara, California. The car was being driven by his young Filipino valet, Garcia Stevenson, who was also killed in the accident . . . and who, according to legend, was getting some very personal service from his boss in the front seat. It wasn't a big load who attended Murnau's funeral—only eleven people showed up, including actor Emil Jannings, Greta Garbo (who would commission a death mask of Murnau that she kept on her desk), and fellow director Fritz Lang, who delivered the eulogy.

WE always knew smoking kills . . . even when the cigar's not lit. Innovative comic Ernie Kovacs (1919–1962) was on his way home from a baby shower, driving his new 1962 Corvair station wagon during a rainstorm when he lost control of the car on a curve and hit a telephone pole. Kovacs was as good a driver as comedic force, so why the accident? Police found an unlit cigar just out of reach, theorizing that Ernie lost control while trying to reach for it while going fifty-five miles per hour. The resulting trauma fractured his skull, smashed his ribs, and ruptured his aorta. Death was instantaneous.

If the only things certain in life are death and taxes, Kovacs was one confident man: When he died ten days before his forty-third birthday, he owed the government several hundred thousand dollars in back taxes—he believed the tax system was unfair and refused to file taxes in protest. His widow, Edie Adams (1927–2008), made television commercials (including ads for Muriel Cigars) and worked arduously to pay off his $600,000 debt.

Kovacs and Adams (who died from complications of pneumonia and cancer) are buried in Forest Lawn Memorial Park in Hollywood Hills, California. (Kovacs is buried with a cigar that Jack Lemmon tucked in his jacket pocket.) Kovacs's grave marker states "Nothing in Moderation. We all loved him." Next to them is the grave of their daughter Mia Susan Kovacs (1959–1982), who, after losing control of her car on Mulholland Drive, ran off the road; the crash ejected her through the sunroof. She was just twenty-two. Her grave insists "We all loved her too."

A Cold Hot Toddy

THERE'S more than a bit of prophetic trivia in the fact that one of Thelma Todd's best roles was opposite the Marx Brothers in the 1931 comedy *Monkey Business*. That title could also serve as the name of her unsolved murder case. The bubbly blond screen comedian (1905–1935) was found dead on the morning of December 16, inside the Pacific Palisades, California, two-car garage of her friend, Jewel Carmen—still in the gown, diamonds, and fur coat she had worn to a party the night before—and slumped inside her chocolate-colored 1934 Lincoln Phaeton convertible.

Police decided that Todd was warming up the car, and died from accidental carbon monoxide poisoning—after all, her skin had turned crimson, a telltale sign. The coagulated blood found around her face and on her dress and inside the car? That, it was determined, had been caused when Hot Toddy's head struck the steering wheel.

Some insisted otherwise, that Todd died at the hands of gangster Charles "Lucky" Luciano after she refused to allow him to use her restaurant for illegal gambling. Others suggested she had been the victim of an extortion attempt, or of abuse from her ex-husband or her lover, who was Jewel's former hubby.

Perhaps most unsettling is what fellow thespian Esther Ralston recalled after going out with Todd the night before she died. "We were all going to see a fortune-teller," Esther said, "and Thelma came out looking pale and quiet, and the next night she was killed."

When Life Bubbles Over

MARIA Africa Gracia Vidal de Santo Silas (1912–1951), whose marquee name was Maria Montez, will be forever known as the Queen of Technicolor. The films she made were as kitschy as they were campy, and so over-the-Technicolor top, most especially 1944's *Cobra Woman*, in which Montez uttered "Geev me the Cobra Chewel!"

Maria's death was not quite as over the top. On September 8, she was taking her ritual midmorning bath. When her sister Adita knocked on the bathroom door, Maria didn't answer; when Adita opened the door, there was

Maria submerged in the steaming water. She had suffered a heart attack just as she stepped into the tub. Firemen spent three hours performing artificial respiration to no avail.

||||||||||||||||||||||||||||||||||||||||||||||||||||||||||||||||||||||||||||||||||||||||||||||||||||||||||||||||||||||||||||||||||

Even though she was a Roman Catholic, Gracie Allen (1902–1964) was buried with Protestant Episcopal rites in a nonsectarian cemetery—Forest Lawn. Smart move by her forward-thinking husband George Burns (1896–1996)—done so that, as a Jew, he could be buried alongside her. Before he died, Burns would visit Gracie's grave once a month, asking her for advice and telling her what he was up to. "If Gracie hears me, fine," he said. "Just talking to her makes me feel good." (Some sources cite Gracie's birth year as 1895 or 1905; we're going with what her hubby gracefully chose for her crypt. Burns once quipped, "I never knew how old Gracie was. I never asked.")

||||||||||||||||||||||||||||||||||||||||||||||||||||||||||||||||||||||||||||||||||||||||||||||||||||||||||||||||||||||||||||||||||

Something's Fishy

WE have one small favor to ask. Pause, momentarily, to remember Eric Fleming (1925–1966), the actor best known for his role as Gil Favor on the long-running small-screen western *Rawhide*. We ask because Fleming's death was pretty ugly. On August 17, the actor arrived in Peru to begin work on a movie. Things were going well until September 28, when his canoe capsized in the swift currents of the Huallaga River. Canoe partner Nic Minardos was able to swim to safety, but Fleming could not . . . his drowning was witnessed by twenty crew and cast members. His body was found several days later, in a remote jungle area, missing some of the flesh that had been dinner for the river's piranha. Fleming had willed his body to the UCLA

Medical Center for research, but his family decided to ship what was left of him to the University of Peru for research purposes. It might have been easier swimming with sharks.

Addicted to Fame

EVERYBODY called her Ollie, especially her husband, actor Jack Pickford (1896–1933), the brother of America's movie sweetheart Mary Pickford. Such a sweet, cute name for sweet, cute Ziegfeld girl Olive Thomas (1894–1920). Today, Thomas is all but forgotten, but her quixotic death keeps her legacy alive. On a second honeymoon to Paris, Jack and Olive went on the town partying, as they were known to do, at several famous bistros in Montparnasse. They returned to the Hotel Ritz at three in the morning and Pickford fell asleep. But Thomas had trouble sleeping. She rummaged through the medicine chest, gulping down a large dose of a mercury bichloride that had been prescribed for her unfaithful husband's chronic syphilis. The label was in French. Thomas, most likely drunk and drugged at the time, thought the bottle contained drinking water or sleeping pills.

She was coherent enough to scream, "Oh, my God! Oh, my God, I'm poisoned!" The suddenly awake and sober Pickford cradled Ollie in his arms while forcing water and egg whites down her throat to induce vomiting. A doctor arrived and pumped her stomach three times. It was too late: Olive Thomas died, at American Hospital in Paris, a few days later. She was buried in Woodlawn Cemetery in the Bronx. A police investigation and an autopsy followed; her death was ruled accidental.

Throughout the rest of his short life, Pickford would be haunted by his wife's death. Some insisted he poisoned her for her insurance money; others believed she committed suicide because of the career-wrecking drug addiction that was taking over his (and her) life. Pickford denied all drugging and drinking stories, repeatedly telling reporters: "Olive and I were the greatest pals on earth. Her death is a ghastly mistake." Pickford died in 1933 of multiple neuritis at thirty-six; from his hospital room, he could see the window of the room in which Ollie died thirteen years earlier.

WE ain't kidding when we say the death of Bobby Driscoll (1937–1968) is one sad story. In 1950, the twelve-year-old received a special Academy Award for "Outstanding Juvenile Performance" for his role in *The Window*, about a boy who witnesses a murder. Then puberty began, his voice deepened, and his skin broke out. The cute little boy was suddenly a Hollywood has-been.

By his late teens, Driscoll was hooked on speed and heroin and arrested repeatedly for drug possession and robbery. After serving a term in California's Chino State Penitentiary, he disappeared into Manhattan's underground. On March 30, three weeks after his thirty-first birthday, two boys playing in a deserted East Village trash-filled and rat-infested tenement found a body, surrounded by religious pamphlets and empty beer bottles. The medical examination determined that the victim had died from heart failure caused by an advanced hardening of the arteries from longtime drug abuse.

The body had no ID, and no one recognized police photos of the corpse. Driscoll's body went unclaimed and was buried in an unmarked pauper's grave in New York City's Potter's Field. Then, late in 1969, some nineteen months after his death, Driscoll's mother asked the FBI and Disney Studios (Driscoll, the first person ever signed to a Disney contract, appeared in their 1946 film *Song of the South*) for help finding the son she assumed was alive. A fingerprint match revealed his tragic fate.

Driscoll's body remains in his unmarked pauper's grave, although his name is engraved on his father's gravestone at Eternal Hills Memorial Park in Oceanside, California.

WHAT'S scarier? His classic performance as Dracula . . . or the fact that Hungarian-born actor Bela Lugosi (1882–1956) was a major morphine addict? By the time he bit the dust of a heart attack while lying on the couch in his Los Angeles apartment, the movie monster was a mere shadow of his former self. Lugosi's body was found with a copy of B-grade film director Ed Wood's next epic, *The Final Curtain*, in his clenched hand. Ah, a movie he could have really sunk his teeth into! Lugosi was buried in Holy Cross Cemetery in Culver City, California, wearing a Dracula cape—the expenses were quietly paid for by fan Frank Sinatra.

FIGHTING for freedom of speech was nothing new to foul-mouthed Lenny Bruce (1925–1966), whose raw language often got him in trouble. Or fired. Or arrested. During a 1964 obscenity charge for using foul language in a Greenwich Village nightclub act, Bruce fired his lawyers and botched the appeal. The conviction on the misdemeanor obscenity charge made it almost impossible for him to get work; he declared bankruptcy and was found dead sitting on the toilet with his pants around his waist, a needle in his arm, and his lifeless body surrounded by drug paraphernalia. Bruce was forty years old. But in 2003, nearly four decades after the comic died, he got the last laugh when on December 23, he was posthumously pardoned by New York governor George E. Pataki, thirty-seven years after being convicted of obscenity. The governor said the posthumous pardon—the first in the state's history—was "a declaration of New York's commitment to upholding the First Amendment." No comment from the dead Bruce, but his daughter Kitty Bruce gushed, "Isn't this wonderful?

Isn't this a great day in America? Boy, has this been nuts or what? This is what America is all about."

Free Weight

NO one could accuse game show icon Arlene Francis of being a dumbbell, except maybe Alvin Rodecker (1900–1960), the man she managed to kill with one. In 1960, the Detroit financier took his wife to New York to celebrate his sixtieth birthday. They had just dropped a wad of money on a fancy French dinner and were at the corner of 57th Street and Park Avenue, underneath the windows of the Ritz Tower, where Francis lived in an eighth-floor apartment. As they walked by the building, Arlene's maid began removing a screen from a window that had been propped into place by a couple of towel-wrapped dumb bells. As the maid went to reach for the eight-pound weights, one rolled down the windowsill, flying through the air like some miniature spaceship and plop! onto Rodecker's head. His wife recalls he had just said, "Holy cow! That was expensive, but it was worth it. We're really celebrating!" The dumbbell cracked his skull, and Rodecker never regained consciousness. He died a day later. Francis was not charged with a crime, but paid the widow Rodecker $175,000. The Ritz Tower coughed up another $10,000.

Doing the Hustle

HE was Hollywood's leading Latin Lover, taking over the crown when Rudolph Valentino died of peritonitis in 1926. Some may say the crown was more of a tiara. Ramon Novarro (1899–1968) was so beautiful that many were quick to call the openly gay hunk "androgynous" . . . even if the 1925 silent epic, and the actor's greatest success, *Ben-Hur*, shows off a very masculine physique.

It all came to a rather brutal end when the actor was murdered (while murmuring a "Hail Mary") by two teen-age brothers, Tom and Paul Ferguson, whom he hired from an escort agency. After Novarro and Paul had sex, he and his brother, thinking the actor had stashed large sums of money in his Laurel Canyon house, brutally beat and tor-tured him for several hours trying to get him to reveal where the (nonexistent) money was hidden. The twenty-two-year-old Paul was relentless, beating Novarro with a silver cane on his back, stomach, and groin until his body was black and blue. As his brother continued the torture, Tom called his girlfriend in Chicago, telling her that they were at Novarro's home. The phone conversation went on for more than forty minutes; at one point Tom put the phone down to check on what was happening. The girl-friend would later tell police she heard "screams in the background." The thugs left the scene of the crime with a twenty-dollar bill taken from the pocket of Novarro's bath-robe. Novarro died as a result of asphyxiation, choking to death on his own blood. It was Halloween.

Police found quite an ugly crime scene. The phrase "Us girls are better than those fagots" was scrawled on a bath-room mirror. They checked Novarro's phone logs and dis-covered the Chicago call. They called the number, and Tom's girlfriend told them everything. Upon their arrest, Paul convinced his younger brother to confess to the crime; he assumed that, as a juvenile, Tom would only face a year or so in jail, whereas Paul could face the gas chamber. So Tom confessed to the murder. But when the court granted the prosecutor's motion to have him tried as an adult, Tom recanted his confession. Brother blamed brother, and even-tually both were sentenced to life imprisonment. They were eventually released on probation, and both were later rearrested for unrelated crimes.

And as for the rumor that the hustlers shoved a dildo,

given to the actor by Valentino, down Novarro's throat . . . it's just a rumor. But Novarro did own a lead dildo that Valentino gave him. We assume he used it as a paper-weight.

||||||||||||||||||||||||||||||||||||||||||||||||||||||||||||||||||||||||||||||||||||||||||||||||||||||||||||||||||

The official county coroner's report states that Marilyn Monroe (1926–1962) was "a 36-year-old well-developed, well-nourished Caucasian female weighing 117 pounds and measuring 65½ inches in length. The scalp is covered with bleach blond hair. The eyes are blue. Fecal contents light brown and formed." She was buried at Los Angeles's Westwood Memorial Park in a sea green Pucci dress, a bouquet of miniature pink roses placed in her hands by former hubby Joe DiMaggio. At the viewing, Joltin' Joe leaned over the corpse, kissed her forehead and reminded her "I love you! I love you! I love you!" Monroe often joked that she wanted her epitaph to read: Here Lies Marilyn Monroe—38-23-36.   ☠

||||||||||||||||||||||||||||||||||||||||||||||||||||||||||||||||||||||||||||||||||||||||||||||||||||||||||||||||||

IF a picture is worth a thousand words, then photos of the dead body of Albert Dekker (1905–1968) could fill volumes. There is perhaps no more puzzling sexually tinged death in the annals of Hollywood history. On May 5, the actor (best known for his role as Dr. Cyclops) and politician (he won a seat in the California State Assembly in 1944) was found dead in his Hollywood home by his fiancée Geraldine Saunders. But he was not just dead—he was naked, kneeling in the bathtub, a noose tightly wrapped around his neck and looped around the shower's curtain rod, handcuffs on his wrists and a blindfold covering his eyes, a ball gag in his mouth. Two hypodermic needles were inserted in his arm. His body was covered in explicit words written in red lipstick. A woman's vagina was drawn on his stomach, and his nipples had been turned into miniature sun rays. His body was starting to turn purple.

What to think? Some thought the six-foot-three, 240-pound Dekker was gay and was accidentally killed by a male hustler. The coroner's take? Dekker had engaged in autoerotic asphyxiation—the act of self-hanging while masturbating—and the act climaxed badly. Very badly. The cause of death was officially listed as "accidental."

||||||||||||||||||||||||||||||||||||||||||||||||||||||||||||||||||||||||||||||||||||||||||||||||||||||||||||||||||||||||

Errol Flynn (1909–1959) was buried at Forest Lawn Memorial Park Cemetery in Glendale, California, with a half-dozen friends—six bottles of whiskey, farewell gifts from his boozing buddies. ☠

||||||||||||||||||||||||||||||||||||||||||||||||||||||||||||||||||||||||||||||||||||||||||||||||||||||||||||||||||||||||

Reel Bad News

HOLLYWOOD'S UNHAPPY FINAL ENDINGS, 1970–2009

Ski Bumming Out

SHE won a Tony for her critically acclaimed role as singer Sally Bowles in the 1998 Broadway revival of *Cabaret*, was a doting wife and mother, a loving daughter and sister, and she might have been a really good skier.

But no one will ever know.

Natasha Richardson (1963–2009) died two days after falling and striking her head on the ground during a private beginner's ski lesson at the Mont Tremblant resort in Quebec. She was not wearing a helmet at the time. It was an "undramatic accident" on the beginner's slope—after the tumble, the conscious actress joked with two ski patrollers and showed no signs of injury. To be safe, they placed her on a rescue toboggan and took her to the bottom of the hill for a closer look. She was alert and showed no sign of confusion, usually a giveaway that something is wrong. Resort staff continued to urge the actress to see a doctor; they even called an ambulance, whose driver was told he wasn't needed so he turned back. Richardson insisted she was fine, signed a waiver releasing the resort from liability, and walked back to her $1,575-per-night suite. Within an hour, she began complaining of a severe headache. Within a day, after visits to two hospitals in Canada, reports began to surface that the actress was brain-dead. Husband Liam Neeson left the set of the film he was shooting in Toronto and arranged for a private jet to take him and his wife to New York's Lenox Hill Hospital.

There was no hope, nothing anyone could do. Neeson; their two sons; Richardson's sister, actress Joely; and Richardson's mother, actress Vanessa Redgrave, agreed to take her off life support. Before the plug was pulled, Vanessa leaned over her daughter's bed, stroked her face, and gently sang "Edelweiss." Then she fainted. An autopsy stated that the cause of death was an "epidural hematoma due to blunt impact to the head"—meaning the fall's impact caused bleeding between her skull and her brain's covering.

Broadway theaters dimmed their lights in her honor. Richardson was laid to rest in Saint Peter's Episcopal Cemetery, a small rural cemetery in Lithgow, New York, close to the grave of her maternal grandmother, actress Rachel Kempson, who died while visiting Richardson and Neeson at their home in nearby Millbrook in 2003. Those attending Richardson's memorial service and graveside service (held under a large green tent so paparazzi couldn't capture the grief) included Ralph Fiennes, Alan Rickman, Laura Linney, Uma Thurman, and Timothy Dalton.

Going into the Dark "Knight"

HE had fame and fortune, but Heath Andrew Ledger (1979–2008) was still hollow. He was struggling with pressures and expectations placed on him by family and friends and the media—and himself. *Brokeback Mountain*, the film in which Ledger played a closeted cowboy, rocketed the Aussie actor to superstardom. He had broken up with the film's costar, Michelle Williams, who he met on the set and with whom he had a daughter, Matilda Rose, born October 28, 2005. "Michelle is my soul mate and we couldn't love each other any more than we do already. We're like two peas in a pod," Ledger said; in 2006, he took a year off from acting to raise Matilda so Michelle could work.

But he came back with a vengeance in 2007, signing up for a number of high profile movie roles. No wonder he could hardly sleep. Ledger admitted that doing back-to-back roles as a Bob Dylanesque singer in *I'm Not There* and as the Joker in *The Dark Knight* ruined his already less-than-perfect sleep patterns. At the time of his death, he was on a break from the London filming of *The Imaginarium of Doctor Parnassus*—costar Christopher Plummer recalled that Ledger had a "terrible, lingering bug, and he couldn't sleep at all. I thought he'd probably got walking pneumonia."

Ledger told a *New York Times* reporter: "Last week I probably slept an average of two hours a night. I couldn't stop thinking. My body was exhausted, and my mind was still going."

And so he began taking Ambien. Among other prescription drugs. Many other prescription drugs.

On January 22, the actor's housekeeper arrived at his Lower Manhattan apartment about 12:30 p.m. She saw Ledger lying on his bed, facedown with a sheet pulled up around his shoulders and snoring. The actor's masseuse arrived about 2:45 p.m. When he had not come out of his bedroom by 3:00, she entered the room and set up the massage table. She shook Ledger, and when he did not respond, she used his cell phone to call actress Mary-Kate Olsen, a friend of Ledger's, in California. Olsen reportedly told her that she would call private security people in New York.

At 3:26 p.m., the masseuse called 911. While on the phone, she tried to perform CPR on Ledger, but he was unresponsive. Medics arrived seven minutes later, about the same time as a private security person summoned by Olsen. Despite their efforts using a cardiac defibrillator, the medics pronounced Ledger dead at 3:36 p.m.

The news shocked everyone. Almost all asked two questions: Why? How?

The answer came two weeks later, when the toxicology reports were revealed. According to the New York City medical examiner's office, "Mr. Heath Ledger died as the result of acute intoxication by the combined effects of oxycodone, hydrocodone, diazepam, temazepam, alprazolam and doxylamine. We have concluded that the manner of death is accident, resulting from the abuse of prescription medications."

Ledger's father released a statement that also served as a warning: "We learned today the combination of doctor-prescribed drugs proved lethal for our boy. Heath's accidental death serves as a caution to the hidden dangers of combining prescription medication, even at low dosage."

A private memorial service was held on February 9, 2008, at Penhros College in Perth, Western Australia, followed by a private wake on Cottesloe Beach attended by family and friends. Michelle Williams was photographed frolicking in the water. Ledger's body was cremated and his ashes were scattered next to the graves of his grandparents at Karrakatta Cemetery and Crematorium in Perth.

For his role as the Joker, Ledger won a "post-humorous" Academy Award, which was accepted by Ledger's mom, dad, and sister. Once the Oscar was officially engraved by the Academy, it was given by the Ledger family to Michelle Williams, who will give it to their daughter when she turns eighteen. Johnny Depp, Jude Law, and Colin Farrell took over playing versions of Ledger's character Tony in *The*

Imaginarium of Doctor Parnassus. They also donated their salaries to Matilda since the actor's old will did not provide for her.

We'll let Ledger get the last words: "I'm not good at future planning," he once said. "I don't know what I'm doing tomorrow. I live completely in the now, not in the past, not in the future. When I die, my money's not gonna come with me. My movies will live on—for people to judge what I was as a person."

||||||||||||||||||||||||||||||||||||||||||||||||||||||||||||||||||||||||||||||||||||||||||||||||||||||||||||||

It happened one night, the death of Oscar-winning legend Claudette Colbert (1903–1996), after she suffered a series of strokes. But when she was alive, the actress made a promise: "I must never think about death. People who think about death are mentally sick." 💀

||||||||||||||||||||||||||||||||||||||||||||||||||||||||||||||||||||||||||||||||||||||||||||||||||||||||||||||

Star Bucks the System

GEE, and we thought having three Diet Cokes a day makes us jittery. In December 1979, after being diagnosed with mesothelioma, an incurable cancer of the lining of the lungs usually related to asbestos exposure, iconic 1960s movie he-man Steve McQueen (1930–1980) underwent surgery to remove several metastatic tumors in his belly. Radiotherapy and chemotherapy followed. McQueen, who loved racing cars, believed he got the cancer from his exposure to asbestos on movie sets, racing suits, and helmets and the asbestos he removed from a ship during his time in the Marines.

When doctors told him the end was near, McQueen refused to accept the fact he would soon make a final great escape. So he made a getaway to Rosarita Beach, Mexico, where he underwent treatments that—well, the word

"unconventional" fits nicely. Under the guidance of ortho-
dontist William Donald Kelley (whose medical license had
been revoked in 1976 after he claimed he had cured his
own pancreatic cancer), McQueen subjected himself to coffee enemas, doses of fifty vitamins and minerals, psycho-
therapy, prayer sessions, massages and shampoos and
intramuscular injections of live sheep and cow cells and
laetrile, a substance extracted from apricot, bitter almond,
and peaches. Kelley's argument was that caffeine stimu-
lates certain nerves in the lower bowel that would then
trigger a neurological reflex making the liver—the body's
main detoxification organ—work more efficiently.

So sure was "Dr. Kelley" of his "treatments" that he publicly announced the actor would be "completely cured
and return to normal life." McQueen believed him and
recorded a message that was aired over Mexican airwaves:
"Mexico is showing the world a new way of fighting cancer
through nonspecific metabolic therapies. Thank you for
helping to save my life."

Not. In late October 1980, a five-pound tumor was discovered in the actor's abdomen. McQueen's American doctors warned him the tumor was inoperable and that his
heart would not withstand the surgery, but the actor refused to listen. On November 6, doctors operated to remove the cancerous mass, as well as others that had formed
in his neck. He withstood the surgery, but he died the next
day of cardiac arrest at a hospital in Juarez. His cremains
were sprinkled over the Pacific Ocean.

Random Acts of Ransom

IT'S something Lucy and Ethel would do. In May 1982, the
urn containing the ashes of Groucho Marx (1890–1977)
were stolen from a sealed crypt at Eden Memorial Park in
Mission Hills, California. The urn reappeared, without

explanation, later that night at the office of Mount Sinai Memorial Park in Glendale less than twelve miles away. So what happened? An angry cemetery employee—and we assume a Groucho groupie—pried off the cover of the niche then took the urn to his home in Burbank, perhaps in deference to Groucho, who once stated, "I would never be caught dead in Burbank."

Groucho's back at rest—Eden Memorial Park officials moved the comedian to a more "remote" location in a room inside the mausoleum, then installed security cameras throughout the cemetery.

What some people won't do to get a little closer to their idols.

ON March 1, 1978, several months after Charles Chaplin (1889–1977) died, his corpse was stolen by a small band of Swiss mechanics. The plot to extort money from his family failed, the thieves were caught, and the Little Tramp's body was recovered eleven weeks later. Chaplin was then reburied under two meters of concrete to prevent further gravenapping.

|||||||||||||||||||||||||||||||||||||||||||||||||||||||||||||||||||||||||||||||||||||||||||||||||||||||

Don't wives ever listen? Sammy Davis Jr. wanted his coffin to be closed—the vain one didn't want anyone to see his cancer-ravaged body. But no, his wife Altovise had an open casket, and hired a photographer to take photos as twenty-five hundred people took one last glance at the one-eyed entertainer. When she discovered that Davis owed millions in back taxes and that the estate was about to go bankrupt, she had Sammy exhumed and removed $70,000 worth of jewelry that had been buried with him! Altovise died from complications of a stroke in 2009 at age sixty-five, the same age Sammy was when he passed. Yes, she was buried next to her husband. No, we're not sure if

she wore any jewels, but after her two-hour memorial service, her pallbearers tossed their white gloves on top of her
coffin. Is this what's known as "lending a final hand?" 💀

IIIIIIIIIIIIIIIIIIIIIIIIIIIIIIIIIIIIIIIIIIIIIIIIIIIIIIIIIIIIIIIIIIIIIIIIIIIIIIIIIIIIIIIIIIIIIIIIIIIIIIIIIIIIIIIIIIIIII

Sex, Lies, and Videotape

TALK about life's little ironies: *Hogan's Heroes* star Bob Crane
(1928–1978) was touring in the stage comedy *Beginner's
Luck* when he was brutally murdered while he slept in his
Scottsdale, Arizona, condo. Crane was bludgeoned to death
with what was most likely a camera tripod, the left side of
his head horribly beaten. To add more insult to a fatal injury: The killer then cut a cord off a VCR and tied a tight
knot around the actor's neck. There was flaky white residue
around his genitals, leading police to believe that Crane had
masturbated or that the killer, after doing the deed, did the
deed. And you thought it was tough being beaten down by
Colonel Klink in a fictional Nazi POW camp each week.

Police insisted "it was a well-planned murder," and they
had no shortage of possible suspects—the most popular
theory was that a boyfriend or husband of one of his many
female costars murdered Crane. Crane craved sex. Two-
ways, three-ways, or four . . . he was a sex addict, into all
forms and variations, and loved dominance and submis-
sion. He videotaped his trysts, often without his partner's
(or partners') knowledge or consent. He kept scrapbooks
and photo albums filled with detailed accounts of his con-
quests; those in the know even say he built S&M dungeons
in the homes of friends. A friend of Crane's named John
Carpenter was eventually arrested and tried for the murder.
Carpenter, a VCR expert and equally interested in sex (he
and Crane often shared women), was indicted for murder
but was acquitted two months later. He died in 1998, main-
taining his innocence until the very end.

Crane was buried in Oakwood Memorial Cemetery in Chatsworth, California, eight days before his fiftieth birthday. In 1999, Crane's wife, actress Sigrid Valdis (who married Crane in 1970 on the set of *Hogan's Heroes*; she portrayed Hilda on the sitcom), had his body exhumed and buried in Los Angeles's Westwood Memorial Park. The grave remained unmarked until 2003. Sigrid joined Crane in eternal sleep in 2007; today it's hard to miss their resting spots: The black gravestones are decorated with "photos" of Crane as Hogan and Valdis as Hilda.

||||||||||||||||||||||||||||||||||||||||||||||||||||||||||||||||||||||||||||||||||||||||||||||||||||||||||||||||||

JOHN BELUSHI (1949–1982)

Final resting place: Abel's Hill Cemetery, Chilmark, Martha's Vineyard

Belushi was found dead, at thirty-three, nude and curled on his right side and horribly discolored on his bed in Bungalow 3 of the Chateau Marmont in Los Angeles. He died from an injection of cocaine and heroin, given to him by former groupie-turned-lover Cathy Smith, who gave an interview to the *National Enquirer* admitting that she shot up Belushi. She was charged with first-degree murder, a charge that was later reduced to involuntary manslaughter. She served eighteen months in jail.

But Belushi ain't where you think he is. The huge boulder marked BELUSHI is a deterrent, a place fans can leave their liquor bottles and cigarette packs and other sundry "souvenirs." His real grave lies several yards from the boulder, and no, we ain't saying exactly where.   ☻

||||||||||||||||||||||||||||||||||||||||||||||||||||||||||||||||||||||||||||||||||||||||||||||||||||||||||||||

Boulevard of Broken Dreams

STEVE Allen (1921–2000), the father of late-night television, was so revered that on the fortieth anniversary broadcast of *The Tonight Show*, Jay Leno knelt down and kissed his ring. What a heartfelt tribute. But what Allen felt in his heart on October 30, we will never know. While driving his Lexus to his son's home, Allen's car was struck by another vehicle backing out of a driveway. Neither driver was apparently injured. Yet shortly after arriving at his son's home, Allen complained that he didn't feel well, and while napping, he suffered a massive heart attack. He was pronounced dead shortly after 8 p.m.; autopsy results concluded that the accident earlier in the day had caused a blood vessel in his chest to rupture, causing blood to leak into the sac surrounding the heart.

WHEN are rich gay men gonna learn: Hire a hustler and you could be done shopping. Forever. Take Italian filmmaker Pier Paolo Pasolini (1922–1975), who was brutally murdered by being run over several times with his own car on a beach in Rome, Italy. A seventeen-year-old hustler named Giuseppe Pelosi was arrested and confessed to the murder. But thirty years later he retracted his confession (claiming he first made it under the threat of violence to his family) and insisted that three people "with a southern accent" had committed the dirty deed. An investigation into Pasolini's death was reopened in 2005, but the murder remains unsolved. No one really knows what happened . . . but it is known that in the months before his death, Pasolini had met with a number of politicians, with whom he shared "certain important secrets." For now, the film has ended, and Pasolini remains buried near his mother in Cimitero di Casarsa in Friuli-Venezia Giulia, Italy, wearing the jersey of a soccer team he helped found.

TO kill a mockingbird is one thing. To kill a noted film director is another. Alan Pakula (1928–1998) was killed in a freakish car accident on the Long Island Expressway in Melville, New York. The car of the driver in front of Pakula struck a metal pipe, which flew through the air and Pakula's windshield. The pipe struck Pakula in the head, causing him to swerve off the road and into a fence. He was killed instantly.

||||||||||||||||||||||||||||||||||||||||||||||||||||||||||||||||||||||||||||||||||||||||||||||||||||||||||||||||||||||||||

Marlene Dietrich so cherished the genius of her friend and costar Orson Welles (1915-1985) that when he died at age seventy in 1985, she declared, "People should cross themselves when they say his name." Welles was found dead in bed, a typewriter balanced on his huge belly. He had been typing a script when he was felled by a massive heart attack.

||||||||||||||||||||||||||||||||||||||||||||||||||||||||||||||||||||||||||||||||||||||||||||||||||||||||||||||||||||||||||

Out-of-Body Experiences

STAR Trek creator Gene Roddenberry (1921–1991) has gone where few men have gone before. When he died, seven grams of his ashes were launched into space by Celestis Inc., the pioneer and global leader in memorial spaceflights. Now that his wife, actress Majel Barrett Roddenberry (1932–2008), has died, Mr. and Mrs. will be reunited. Of sorts. Says their son Gene Jr.: "We have planned a very compelling future memorial service for my mother and father. Fulfilling a pledge made to Majel in 1995, Celestis Inc.

will launch [fourteen grams of] my mother and my father together, side-by-side, on an infinite journey into deep space aboard their Voyager Memorial Spaceflight Service. The spacecraft is currently planned for launch in 2012 and it will carry their spirits, their memories, and the message of their life's work into the cosmos." The fee? A cool $37,500. This includes invitations to the launch and memorial services, a custom-made, professionally produced DVD of the launch and memorial activities, inscription of the participant's name and message on a special plaque included in the spacecraft, and complimentary scattering of the balance of remaining cremated remains at sea near the launch site.

Celestis has also "buried" someone on the moon for the first time—seven grams of Dr. Eugene Shoemaker (1928–1997), a pioneer in the exploration of the solar system, have resided in a crater on the south lunar pole since the NASA *Lunar Prospector* landed on the moon at 4:52 a.m. on July 31, 1999. NASA called the memorial "a special honor for a special human being."

DON'T even think of trying to find the grave of Walden Robert "Bobby" Cassotto (1936–1973), otherwise known as Bobby Darin. The teen idol suffered cruelly from heart problems. After a dentist visit, he didn't take prescribed medication and developed blood poisoning that weakened his body and clotted one of his heart valves. He died after eight hours of surgery to repair that and another faulty heart valve. He donated his body to the University of California at Los Angeles for medical research.

||||||||||||||||||||||||||||||||||||||||||||||||||||||||||||||||||||||||||||||||||||||||||||||||||||||||||||||||||||||||||||||

Where there's a will, there's a way: Though she weighed just seventy-five pounds, couldn't keep food down, and was on an intravenous morphine drip, on

January 10, Audrey Hepburn (1929–1993), two nurses in tow, paid one last visit to the beloved garden of her Swiss home. "I want to feel alive one more time before I die," she told them. Upon learning of her death, Liz Taylor wept, stating that "God has a most beautiful new angel."   💀

IIIIIIIIIIIIIIIIIIIIIIIIIIIIIIIIIIIIIIIIIIIIIIIIIIIIIIIIIIIIIIIIIIIIIIIIIIIIIIIIIIIIIIIIIIIIIIIIIIIIIIIIIIIIIIIIIIIIIIIIIIIIIIIIIIIII

Newman's Own

THE lengths—and lies—some press agents will go to to protect clients. Take the case of blue-eyed beauty Paul Newman (1925–2008). In January 2008, the *National Enquirer* reported that the eighty-three-year-old actor had undergone surgery for cancer. Enter Newman's rep, Warren Cowan, who denied the report by quoting the actor: "I'm being treated for athlete's foot and hair loss." Two months later, when Newman didn't show up for a charity event benefiting his Hole in the Wall Gang Camps for kids fighting cancer and serious blood diseases, Cowan let loose with: "He's having back problems. He has to stay off his feet for a couple of weeks." Newman really had people wondering when he withdrew from a highly publicized gig directing a stage production of *Of Mice and Men*.

That's because Newman, who once said that he was afraid his gravestone would say "Here lies Paul Newman, who died a failure because his eyes turned brown" and/or "Here lies the old man who wasn't a part of his time," was dying. After receiving cancer treatments at a New York hospital, Newman returned to his Westport, Connecticut, home, with wife, actress Joanne Woodward, and their three daughters by his side. "The trick of living is to slip on and off the planet with the least fuss you can muster," he once said.

Newman slipped off on September 26, and was cremated

after a private funeral service. With little fuss, his friends and family celebrated his life at the Dressing Room, the Westport restaurant Newman owned.

||||||||||||||||||||||||||||||||||||||||||||||||||||||||||||||||||||||||||||||||||||||||||||||||||||

His films live on forever, even if he did refuse the Oscar for his role in *Patton*. Yet George C. Scott (1927–1999) remains buried in an unmarked grave. Maybe his belief in not competing with other actors is the reason . . . his body lies in the plot immediately to the left of Walter Matthau's grave at Westwood Memorial Park, a blank headstone marking the spot.   ☠

||||||||||||||||||||||||||||||||||||||||||||||||||||||||||||||||||||||||||||||||||||||||||||||||||||

Mac Attack

HE was a man of many laughs, but nothing was funny about the death of Bernard Jeffrey McCullough (1957–2008). The comedian, best known for his role in the big-screen *Ocean's Eleven* trilogy and his long-running TV program *The Bernie Mac Show*, suffered from sarcoidosis, a disease that caused tiny clumps of inflammatory cells to grow in his lungs and various organs throughout his body. In 2005, Mac claimed the disease was in remission. Two years later, on David Letterman's late-night talk show, the comic said he would soon retire.

But something funny was going on. On August 1, Mac was admitted to Chicago's Northwestern Memorial Hospital with pneumonia; the next day, a family spokesperson said that Mac was in "very, very critical" condition. Yet his publicist reported that the comedian was in "stable condition," expected to make "a full recovery," was responding well to treatment, and his release from the hospital was "expected in weeks." A week later, early on the morning of August 9, Mac was dead.

Mac's life was surrounded by visits from the Grim Reaper: His mother died of cancer when he was sixteen; one brother died in infancy, another of a heart attack in his twenties. But Mac's memorial service at Chicago's House of Hope was anything but sad. More than seven thousand people attended his funeral, and the reminiscences, recollections, and laughs flowed as freely as the tears. Many famous friends and other kings of comedy were there, including Steve Harvey, Chris Rock, and Cedric the Entertainer; ironically, one friend, Isaac Hayes, with whom Mac was working on the movie *Soul Men*, could not make it—he died one day after Mac.

Perhaps the most unique memorial came from the Chicago White Sox—Mac's favorite team—who gave his widow, Rhonda, a baseball jersey bearing her hubby's name and the number one.

President Obama was a fan of Mac's—to a point. When Mac performed at a $2,300-a-head July 2008 fund-raiser to help elect Barack, his ten-minute act was filled with so many offensive comments that the presidential hopeful said, "By the way, Bernie, you got to clean up your act."

He's buried in a crypt at Washington Memory Gardens Cemetery in Homewood, Illinois, with a promise that "we'll love you forever."

That's Why They're Called "Warning Labels"

WE cannot lose sight of the irony that by the time Brad Renfro (1982–2008) was discovered at age ten and cast in *The Client*, his only previous acting experience was as a drug dealer in an antidrug stage production put on by his school. And it was the Knoxville (Tennessee) Police Department, who knew of the youngster's reputation as a troublemaker, who led the film's casting director to the boy.

Less than sixteen years later, it was all over.

MERV GRIFFIN (1925–2007)

Final resting place: Westwood Memorial Park, Los Angeles, California

The answer is: At the time of his death, on August 12 of prostate cancer, he was a billionaire.

And the question: Who was Mervyn Edward Griffin Jr.?

He may have begun his career as a $100-a-week radio and big band singer, but Griffin made it big as the host of his talk show, and really big as the creator of such TV game shows as *Jeopardy!* and *Wheel of Fortune,* the latter of which caused the largest vowel-movement in show-biz history. In the early 1990s, he was sued for $200 million by a former male employee, on palimony charges, and for $11.5 million by former *Dance Fever* host Deney Terrio for sexual harassment. Both cases were eventually dismissed. Merv was letter-perfect at evading questions about his sexuality, telling the *New York Times,* "I tell everybody that I'm a quartresexual. I will do anything with anybody for a quarter." 💀

Renfro was a troubled youth—he was charged with marijuana and cocaine possession in 1998; when he was eighteen, a judge sentenced him to two years' probation and ordered him to pay more than $4,000 for repairs on a yacht he tried to steal.

The waters would only get rougher. In 2005, the actor was arrested in a Los Angeles Skid Row police sting in which he was charged with possessing heroin; Renfro eventually pled guilty to the charge, served ten days in jail, and was sentenced to three years' probation. A few weeks earlier, he was charged with driving under the influence and two counts of driving with a suspended license.

In June 2007 Renfro violated his probation by not enrolling in a long-term drug treatment program. A year later he was dead. Renfro died at his Los Angeles apartment; his girlfriend remembers Renfro drinking that night and remembers hearing him snoring. But the next morning she found him neither drinking nor snoring. Or breathing. She called 911, and Renfro was declared dead at the scene at about 9 a.m. If he had only been an apt pupil and paid attention when Nancy Reagan said just say no.

More than six hundred people attended his three-hour funeral; his casket was closed and all that reminded people of the man inside was a simple arrangement of red, white, and yellow flowers and a color photograph of the actor in his younger, happier, and cleaner days. (Shortly before he died, Renfro had "F— All Y'all" tattooed across his back.) Renfro's great-uncle, Michael Earl, officiated. "Was Brad perfect?" he asked during the eulogy. "Well, I can tell you I'm not. Are you? And I'm gonna see him again. Oh, what a reunion! It's not goodbye, but it's see you later."

A few weeks before he died, Renfro spent time with his secret son, listed as "Y Renfro" in published obituaries. The actor's resting spot is not so secret: He's buried in Red House Cemetery in Blaine, Tennessee.

ANNA Nicole Smith (1967–2007), that gold-digging Marilyn wannabe, was so distraught over the sudden drug overdose of her twenty-year-old son Daniel (1986–2006) that at his funeral she had officials open the coffin so she could climb inside. She needn't have asked. Five months later, when the ex-Playmate died, she was buried alongside him in Lakeview Memorial Gardens and Mausoleums in Nassau, Bahamas. Her eight-page autopsy report (filed under her real name, Vickie Lynn Marshall) states that her death was "accidental" and the primary cause was "an acute combined drug intoxication." It also details her breast implant scarring, her tattoos, and various bits of medical minutiae: "multiple hairs" were pulled from "various parts" of her scalp, the nails of her left hand were "cut and preserved," her brain was removed and weighed 1,300 grams, her vagina was "normally wrinkled" and contained "no foreign matter," and her cyst and abscess-riddled buttocks were dissected. Ouch!

||||||||||||||||||||||||||||||||||||||||||||||||||||||||||||||||||||||||||||||||||||||||||||||||||||||

When her daughter Maria Riva buried Marlene Dietrich (1901–1992), she wasn't taking any chances: Lili Marlene was buried in a mahogany casket with a wooden crucifix, a St. Christopher's medal, a Star of David, and a locket containing photos of the actress's grandkids.   ☻

||||||||||||||||||||||||||||||||||||||||||||||||||||||||||||||||||||||||||||||||||||||||||||||||||||||

Sizzling Careers

JACK Cassidy (1927–1976) had turned bitter in his old age. And he wasn't even that old. He was jealous of son David's success (the younger Cassidy was a huge teen hunk in *The Partridge Family*), and he was angry that he had turned down the role of Ted Baxter in *The Mary Tyler Moore Show*.

On the early morning of December 12, the forty-nine-year-old actor fell asleep on the couch of his West Hollywood apartment . . . smoking a cigarette. Suddenly, Cassidy's career was hot. Real hot. The entire top floor of the apartment building caught on fire. A hundred residents had to be evacuated and five fire departments showed up to put out the blaze. One body remained. The charred remains of Cassidy were discovered just inside the door of the apartment. So badly burned was Cassidy that he could only be positively identified through dental records and two pieces of jewelry he was wearing, a signet ring and a religious bracelet.

Yes, he was cremated, his ashes scattered at sea.

SHE was dark and smoldering, just like her death. Teresa Graves (1948–2002) was known for her many appearances on *Rowan & Martin's Laugh-In* and as the sexy, sassy, and smart undercover police officer in the hit TV series *Get Christie Love!*—the first African American female to star as a detective in her own series.

The blaze originated in a faulty space heater in the bedroom of the South Los Angeles home she shared with her mother. Firefighters found the actress unconscious, and she died, at fifty-three, at a nearby hospital. Her ashes were scattered at sea. Hopefully she is at peace. Graves, frustrated with the business, had quit acting to become a Jehovah's Witness. We would have let her in if she came a-knockin' on our door.

||||||||||||||||||||||||||||||||||||||||||||||||||||||||||||||||||||||||||||||||||||||||||||||||||||||||||||||||||||||||||||||

It took a long time, but John Wayne (1907–1979) finally got a grave marker. On his deathbed—the actor died of stomach cancer on June 11—the Duke converted to Roman Catholicism and requested his tombstone to read, "Feo, Fuerte, y Formal," a Spanish phrase meaning "ugly, strong, and dignified." Instead, his grave at Pacific View Memorial Park remained unmarked for twenty years. Today it bears a quotation from his 1971 *Playboy* interview: "Tomorrow is

the most important thing in life. Comes into us at midnight very clean. It's perfect when it arrives and it puts itself in our hands. It hopes we've learned something from
yesterday." ☻

||||||||||||||||||||||||||||||||||||||||||||||||||||||||||||||||||||||||||||||||||||||||||||||||||||||||||||||||||||

Flying the Unfriendly Skies

MICHAEL Findlay (1938–1977), along with his wife, Roberta, was considered the king of sexploitation films; he
eagerly welcomed the moniker of "the most notorious
filmmaker in the annals of sexploitation." It's fitting that
his crowning glory was his decapitation. On May 16, Findlay was killed in a helicopter accident on the roof of the
Pan Am Building in New York City. He was on his way to
Kennedy Airport to connect with a Paris-bound flight; it
was in Paris that Findlay was planning to demonstrate his
new 3-D camera to potential backers. No such luck. Findlay
and three other passengers were about to board the copter,
when the landing support collapsed and the copter fell on
its side. The spinning rotor blades decapitated Findlay and
killed three other passengers. A woman on Madison Avenue was also killed when she was hit by a detached rotor
blade. Snuff said.

IT really was a scene straight out of *The Twilight Zone*. Actor
Vic Morrow (1929–1982) along with two young children,
My-Ca Dinh Le, seven, and Renee Shin-Yi Chen, six, were
filming a key scene of the 1982 flick *Twilight Zone: The Movie*.
And something went wrong. Very wrong. The helicopter
pursuing them in the scene lost control and the blades went
a-whirling. Morrow and Le were decapitated; Chen was
crushed underneath the helicopter's landing skid.

To get around child labor laws, the children were illegally hired and working without supervision. The film's director John Landis and other defendants (including producer Steven Spielberg and pilot Dorsey Wingo) were eventually acquitted of involuntary manslaughter and child endangerment. The parents of Le and Chen sued and settled out of court for $2 million each; Morrow's children also sued and settled for an undisclosed amount.

||||||||||||||||||||||||||||||||||||||||||||||||||||||||||||||||||||||||||||||||||||||||||||||||||||||||||||||||||||||||||||||||||||||||||||||||||

MEL BLANC (1908–1989)

Final resting place: Hollywood Forever Cemetery, Hollywood, California

Blanc provided the voice of Daffy Duck for more than fifty-two years and for hundreds and hundreds of other cartoon creations, including Porky Pig, Yosemite Sam, Wile E. Coyote, and Barney Rubble.

Bugs Bunny remains the fourteen-karat favorite. When it was decided that Bugs would munch on carrots, sound technicians tried everything from turnips to celery to potatoes, but the snap, the sound, wasn't the same. So every time Bugs chomped, Blanc chomped—then promptly spit out the carrot pieces.

Blanc died on July 10 of heart disease and emphysema, and is buried in a grave whose inscription, "That's All Folks," was stipulated in his will.   💀

||||||||||||||||||||||||||||||||||||||||||||||||||||||||||||||||||||||||||||||||||||||||||||||||||||||||||||||||||

This River Ran Deep

RIVER Phoenix (1970–1993) was a dedicated animal-rights activist, an environmentalist, and a die-hard vegan—he wore no leather and cared so much about the diminishing rain forest that he bought acres and acres of it in Costa Rica to save it from development.

But by the time Phoenix had costarred in hits such as *Indiana Jones and the Last Crusade*, he was changed. Moody and restless, he had all but abandoned acting, moved back to Florida to be near his family, and, with his sister Rain, formed the rock band Aleka's Attic. But through it all, he always insisted that he believed in clean living: "I don't see any point or any good in drugs that are as disruptive as cocaine. I never tried heroin. I tried alcohol and most of the others when I was 15, and got it out of the way—finished with the stuff."

Yeah, right. And Marilyn was a real blonde.

Come 1993, Phoenix was back in Los Angeles, working on the film *Dark Blood* and set to begin filming the long-awaited big-screen version of Anne Rice's *Interview with the Vampire*. On the evening of October 30, Phoenix went to the Viper Room, a nightclub on Sunset Boulevard owned by Johnny Depp. A few minutes before 1 a.m., River had been in the bathroom doing drugs. Someone offered him a snort of high-grade Persian Brown; the actor immediately began trembling and shaking. He screamed and vomited. Someone gave him a Valium. The actor staggered over to his girlfriend, actress Samantha Mathis, and his sister Rain, complaining that he couldn't breathe before briefly passing out. Going outside for air, he collapsed on the sidewalk and began having seizures. A paparazzo called 911; so did River's brother Joaquin. Rain emerged from the club and threw herself on her brother in an attempt to stop the seizures. His last words? "No paparazzi. I want anonymity."

Paramedics rushed Phoenix to Cedars-Sinai Medical Center. His skin was dark blue, but he was still alive. Emergency Room doctors tried to revive him—they even inserted a pacemaker—but it was too late. It was Halloween but this was no trick. River Phoenix was pronounced dead at 1:51 a.m. He was twenty-three years old. The autopsy showed that River was riddled with drugs—lethal levels of cocaine and heroin, Valium, marijuana, and crystal meth. The official cause of death: "acute multiple drug ingestion."

Only sixty mourners showed up at the funeral home for the viewing. At his mother's request, the actor's shoulder-length hair was cut and placed beside him in his casket. (His blond tresses had been dyed black for the film on which he was working.) He was dressed in a black T-shirt emblazoned with the logo of his band. His mother also placed a single carnation in the coffin; as the mourners passed his coffin, many placed notes and necklaces inside. A reporter broke into the funeral home and took a picture of Phoenix in his coffin, which was sold to the *National Enquirer* for $5,000. He was cremated; his ashes were scattered at his family's ranch in Florida. *Dark Blood* was never released (it was a mere eleven days short of completion when Phoenix died) but die-hard Phoenix fans can find snatches of it on YouTube. Christian Slater took over Phoenix's role in *Interview with the Vampire*, then kindly donated his $250,000 salary to two of Phoenix's favorite charities.

Still, if reincarnation does exist, will he rise out of the ashes like a Phoenix?

JACK LEMMON (1925–2001)

Final resting place: Westwood Memorial Park, Los Angeles, California

Lemmon appeared in some sixty films, earning eight Oscar nominations and winning the coveted gold-plated statuette twice, for *Mister Roberts* (1955) and for *Save the Tiger* (1973).

These days, Lemmon, who died of cancer on June 27, stars in . . . nothing except B6, the exact spot of earth marking his grave in the Chapel Garden section of Westwood Memorial Cemetery. He is buried next to his friend and frequent costar Walter Matthau, most certainly the cemetery's oddest couple.   ☺

Sordid Lives (and Deaths)

IF you don't know the name or face, you know the throat. Linda Susan Boreman (1949–2002), better known as Linda Lovelace, was most famous for her performance of deep throat fellatio in the 1972 hardcore mega-hit porn film *Deep Throat*. The freckle-faced Linda, who would later denounce her pornography career (she claimed she was forced into it by her sadistic first husband), insisted she never made a penny for her work though the film grossed more than $600 million. Now that's tough to swallow. Linda suffered massive trauma and internal injuries in an auto accident near Denver on April 3. The accident left her in a coma, and she was taken off life support and died about 3 p.m.

SHE, Jackie Curtis (1947–1985), was born a he (John Holder Jr.), and he/she became one of Andy Warhol's greatest superstars. When Curtis died of a heroin overdose at the age of thirty-eight, she was dressed as a man in his coffin— handsome, if a bit effete, in a dark suit, his hair slicked back and a white flower on his lapel. Those who wanted a more suitable souvenir could take one of the photographs of Jackie in drag that were on a nearby table. Warhol didn't show (he sent flowers), and friends filled the casket with photographs and mementos of a cross-dressing career, including packs of Kool cigarettes, a cocktail shaker full of martinis, even a magic wand. The dead body was liberally sprinkled with glitter; later, after Curtis was interred in Rose Hill Memorial Park in Putnam Valley, New York, friends covered his grave with so much red glitter that one person recalls "it could be seen from the highway."

And They Did Not Live Happily Ever After

SMALL-SCREEN hunk Jon-Erik Hexum (1957–1984), so young, so pretty, so buff, died on the set of his TV series *Cover Up*. On October 12, a bored Hexum playfully placed a prop gun against his temple and joked, "Let's see if I got one for me!" He pulled the trigger and the joke backfired . . . literally. The blank-loaded .44 Magnum's charge blew a quarter-size piece of Hexum's skull into his brain. He was rushed into surgery, but despite five hours of work, the hospital's chief surgeon explained there was no hope, and he

NICHOLAS RICHARD CONTE (1910–1975)

RICHARD NICHOLAS PETER CONTE
1910 – 1975 – ?
ACTOR-WRITER-PAINTER-COMPOSER-POET
A MAN OF MANY TALENTS AND GRACES
LOVED BY A THOUSAND UNKNOWN FACES
BUT HE LOVED BEST AND IS LOVED MOST
BY HIS LOVER-FRIEND-MOTHER-CHILD-WIFE
SHIRLEE COLLEEN
NICKY-THE MASTER OF GENTLE WORDS
AND DEEDS
YOU SHARED SO MUCH, GAVE SO MUCH-RECEIVED
SO LITTLE, UNTIL NOW WHEN ALL IS YOURS
FLY WITH JOY THAT I MAY GREET YOU ON THE
WINGS OF OUR FRIEND, THE BIRD OF BLUE
MAY THE FATES BE KINDER IN OUR NEXT
LIFE AND TAKE US BOTH TOGETHER-TO BE-
AT LONG LAST COMPLETE.

Final resting place: Westwood Memorial Park, Los Angeles, California

While Conte never achieved major star status, he is still considered one of film noir's greatest players. He was so good that he was one of many actors seriously considered by Paramount for the title role of Don Corleone in *The Godfather*. Marlon Brando finally won the plum assignment and Conte was cast in the role of his rival, Don Barzini.

Conte died of a heart attack on April 15 at age sixty-five. Even those who don't remember him pause at his gravestone—that's because Conte's strong belief in the afterlife is clearly reflected on the marker. When will he be back? Is he already back? The question (and question mark) remains.   ☻

was pronounced dead at 7:30 p.m. Ironically, Hexum's *Cover Up* costar, Jennifer O'Neill, accidentally shot herself two years earlier; when she heard of Hexum's death, she said, "This is a personal loss, and a loss for everyone." Though brain-dead, Hexum was flown to San Francisco, where his heart was implanted into the body of a dying, thirty-six-year-old Las Vegas businessman. (His corneas and kidneys were also donated.) His mother Gretha cremated what was left, sprinkling the ashes into the Pacific, not far from one of Hexum's favorite beach jogging spots.

ONE of the original members of the Rat Pack, Peter Lawford (1923–1984) did mouse around when it came to living life. He loved to drink, eat, and fornicate, dallying with both men and women. Lawford died in a Los Angeles hospital on Christmas Eve of cardiac arrest, complicated by kidney and liver failure from years of drug and alcohol abuse. His body was cremated and the ashes were interred at Westwood Memorial Park. None of the Rat Packers—Frank Sinatra, Joey Bishop, or Sammy Davis Jr.—attended.

Then things got a bit shaky. In May 1988, the Lawford estate was reminded they owed $10,000 to the cemetery—it was time to pay up or pull out. Lawford's widow and fourth wife, Patricia Seaton, not wanting to pay the bill, had Lawford's ashes removed and scattered off the coast of California, an event she invited the *National Enquirer* to cover.

WHAT if they gave a funeral and no one came? Well, not no one. People did attend the funeral of Betty Hutton (1921–2007): a few friends, one Paramount Studios executive, and lots of fans who came to gawk. The only celebrity in sight was Hutton, and even she wasn't visible since she had been cremated and her ashes tucked in an urn. Even her three daughters didn't attend.

It was a sad finale for an entertainer, who used to bring 'em in by the thousands; by the time she died of colon cancer on March 11, she was penniless, her career and life shattered by drugs. Hutton spent the last years of her life living in an apartment complex in Palm Springs, California, that was owned by a gay couple. They paid her rent, bought her food and clothes, and protected her from the outside world. A few days after her burial, the men began selling her possessions on eBay. A bright pink mono-grammed bathrobe (still with tags! never worn!) fetched a few bucks, plus postage.

HE played TV's quintessential dad, Mike Brady, on *The Brady Bunch* for six years, yet few people knew that Robert Reed (1932–1992) was gay and would die of bladder and colon cancer, both complications from AIDS. Florence Henderson, who portrayed his small-screen spouse Carol, recalls, "Bob never mentioned the word 'AIDS.' Two weeks before he died, he called me and said, 'Florence, I told you I'd be honest. I am not going to make it, and I am fine with it. If I can just ask you one favor—will you call the kids [the young performers who played the "bunch"]?' I called them, and all of them fell apart." Reed was cremated and is buried in Memorial Park Cemetery in Skokie, Illinois. His simple gravestone reads: "Goodnight Sweet Prince."

LUCILLE Ball (1911–1989) was glad that we all loved Lucy, but even when she was alive, she felt dead. "All the praise I hear—people calling me superstar and legend and all the god-damned honors I get—makes me feel like I'm reading my own obituary. Award-giving is an aging process and it makes me feel like I'm dead. Damn, I didn't want to outlive my original order of henna!" America's greatest funny girl died of a ruptured aorta at age seventy-seven, a week after having undergone eight-hour emergency surgery for a dis-secting aortic aneurysm. She was cremated and buried with her mother in the Columbarium of Radiant Love at Forest Lawn in Hollywood Hills. In 2002, her children, Lucie Arnaz and Desi Arnaz Jr., disinterred their famous mother and re-buried her in the family plot at Lake View Cemetery in Jamestown, New York, where Ball's mother, father, brother, and grandparents are buried. (It's also a great marketing gimmick, since the Lucille Ball–Desi Arnaz Center is a couple minutes' drive away.) The black tombstone declares that Lucy has "come home." The back of the stone has the familiar "I Love Lucy" heart framing the word "Ball."

IIIIIIIIIIIIIIIIIIIIIIIIIIIIIIIIIIIIIIIIIIIIIIIIIIIIIIIIIIIIIIIIIIIIIIIIIIIIIIIIIIIIIIIIIIIIIIIIIIIIIIIIIIIIIIIIIIIIIIIIII

JOAN HACKETT (1934–1983)

Final resting place: Hollywood Forever Cemetery, Hollywood, California.

Though she was wracked with ovarian cancer, Hackett checked herself out of the hospital so she could host a wedding party at her Beverly Hills home for her pals Carrie Fisher and Paul Simon. The former wife of Richard Mulligan died on October 8 at 9:15 p.m. She so loved to get her beauty sleep that we leave her quietly resting in the arms of Morpheus, in Crypt 2314 in the Sanctuary of Faith.

IIIIIIIIIIIIIIIIIIIIIIIIIIIIIIIIIIIIIIIIIIIIIIIIIIIIIIIIIIIIIIIIIIIIIIIIIIIIIIIIIIIIIIIIIIIIIIIIIIIIIIIIIIIIIIIIIIIIIIIIII

EVEN in death, Greta Garbo (1905–1990) *vants* to be alone. When she died, Garbo bequeathed an estate of twenty million dollars to her niece and sole heir, Gray Reisfield. (Despite lovers of both sexes and a list of suitors as long as the credits to any of her films, Garbo never married.) The actress was cremated and the ashes kept at a New York City mortuary until 1999 when Reisfield finally decided to inter them in Garbo's native land, in the same cemetery where Garbo's parents rest.

Or did she? Some say Garbo never made a final return to Sweden. Stories abound that the tombstone is really a cenotaph, a courteous nod to the country that many felt she abandoned when she went to Hollywood in the 1920s.

As for the Associated Press photos and TV footage of the intimate (thirty-five people attended) burial ceremony? Some say they are a ruse, sort of in the same way rumors fly that man never really landed on the moon.

Truth be told, Garbo is indeed buried at Skogskyrkogården, a huge cemetery outside of Stockholm. *Very* buried: Her family was so afraid someone would steal her ashes that Garbo is buried two meters deep, her urn in a block of concrete.

llllllllllllllllllllllllllllllllllllllllllllllllllllllllllllllllllllllllllllllllllllllllllllllllllllll

RODNEY DANGERFIELD (1921–2004)

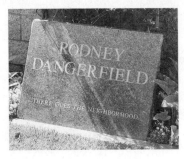

Final resting place: Westwood Memorial Park, Los Angeles, California

You gotta love a guy who, at eighty-two, was still smoking pot. The funny man was, indeed, a pothead since he was twenty-one. During the Reagan years, he once got stoned at the White House; in 2002, after being wheeled into the intensive care unit during a heart attack scare, Dangerfield lit up a joint in the bathroom! At the end of his life, the comic was a "legal pothead," having received doctor's orders to smoke the stuff to control his high blood pressure. Dangerfield died on October 5 from complications after heart-valve replacement surgery. And he finally gets respect.   ☻

llllllllllllllllllllllllllllllllllllllllllllllllllllllllllllllllllllllllllllllllllllllllllllllllllllll

* * *

THE last people to visit Susan Hayward (1917–1975) when she was alive were some of Hollywood's biggest names: Barbara Stanwyck, Greta Garbo, and Katharine Hepburn. Hayward died at 2 p.m. on March 14 after suffering a massive seizure. She was clutching a crucifix that had been blessed and given to her by Pope John XXIII.

Glenda Farrell (1904–1971) is the only actress buried in the U.S. Military Academy Post Cemetery in West Point, New York, not for her on-screen work but for her off-screen accomplishments. She was married to Dr. Henry Ross, a graduate of the school who's lying in a separate grave beside her.

The Write Stuff

Getting to the Heart of the Matter

FRANKENSTEIN creator Mary Wollstonecraft Shelley (1797–1851) knew how to get to the heart of life's matters. Her hubby, English romantic poet Percy Bysshe Shelley (1792–1822), died at sea; when his badly decomposed body finally washed up on the shore of the Tyrrhenian Sea, quarantine laws demanded he be burned on the beach. Mary did not attend the funeral, but she still got a piece of the action: Her husband's heart was snatched from the funeral pyre by fellow writer Edward Trelawny, who gifted it to the grieving widow. Trelawny was good with the words—he recalled that when his pal was found, "the face and hands, and parts of the body not protected by the dress, were fleshless."

On the first anniversary of Mary's death, a box on her desk was opened by family members, who found locks of her dead children's hair, a copy of Percy's poem "Adonaïs," and the remains of his heart.

Easy Off(ed)

MOTHER knows best. When noted bipolar poet Sylvia Plath (1932–1963) decided to take the final path, she made sure her two children would be safe. Before turning on the gas jets in her London kitchen, she left them bread and milk, cracked opened a window in their bedroom, and placed wet towels at the foot of their door to prevent the toxic fumes from reaching them. Then on the morning of February 11, Plath, depressed over her husband's infidelities, stuck her head deep into the bowels of the oven. The Plath passings didn't end there: On March 16, 2009, Plath's forty-seven-year-old son, Nicholas Hughes (1962–2009) hanged himself in his Alaska home—forty-six years after his mom's suicide and almost forty years to the day after his father's mistress, poet Assia Wevill (1927–1969), killed herself and her four-year-old daughter Shura in a copycat suicide. Assia gave her daughter some sleeping pills, popped some herself, sealed off the kitchen windows and door, and turned on the gas.

||||||||||||||||||||||||||||||||||||||||||||||||||||||||||||||||||||||||||||||||||||||||||||||||||||

James Fixx (1932–1984) turned the sport of running into an art. Many credit his 1977 bestseller, *The Complete Book of Running*, with jump-starting America's fitness revolution. Is it any wonder he died of a heart attack while running? ☠

||||||||||||||||||||||||||||||||||||||||||||||||||||||||||||||||||||||||||||||||||||||||||||||||||||

FRANK O'Hara (1926–1966) had the write stuff, but died in the wrong place. The provocative postwar poet died in a rather freakish accident. In the early morning hours of July 24, the openly gay O'Hara had been cruising for sexual companions in the dunes of Fire Island Pines when he was struck and seriously injured by a man speeding by in a beach vehicle. He died the next day of a ruptured liver at the age of forty, and was buried in the Green River Cemetery in East Hampton, Long Island. What a blow to the literary world.

NOTED English playwright Joe Orton (1933–1967) knew how to write. He didn't, however, know how to choose Mr. Right. He chose fellow writer and sometime actor Kenneth Halliwell (1926–1967), who on August 9, 1967, bludgeoned his thirty-four-year-old lover to death with nine hammer blows to the head. Then, just to be safe, Halliwell committed suicide, gulping twenty-two Nembutals and washing them down with canned grapefruit juice. The bodies were discovered the following morning by the chauffeur. Police determined that the forty-one-year-old Halliwell—who left a suicide note stating all would be explained if they read Orton's diaries "especially the latter part" (which detailed Orton's promiscuity)—died first because Orton's body was still warm.

Orton was cremated at the Golders Green Crematorium; his ashes and those of Halliwell are buried in an unmarked grave in the garden of the crematorium.

IT'S a talk show host's worst nightmare. There was James Rodale (1898–1971), businessman, publisher, and one of the world's leading experts on organic farming and natural food, chitchatting with Dick Cavett and claiming that "I'm so healthy that I expect to live on and on." Less than ten minutes later, as Cavett was interviewing his second guest, Rodale closed his eyes, dropped his head, and let out a snore. Cavett, ever the quip-master, asked, "Are we boring you, Mr. Rodale?" It was only after two medical interns scrambled onto the stage, loosened his shirt and his pants, and began resuscitation that Dick and the audience learned the truth: The world's healthiest man had just died of a heart attack.

||||||||||||||||||||||||||||||||||||||||||||||||||||||||||||||||||||||||||||||||||||||||||||||||||||||||||||||||||

Erma Bombeck (1927–1996)—the writer who offered such pithy punch lines as "The only reason I would take up jogging is so that I could hear heavy breathing again"— would see the humor in her husband's final act of rock-solid kindness. After being diagnosed with a liver ailment, she underwent a kidney transplant, dying from complications of the operation. Though she was buried in the family plot in Centerville, Ohio, her husband wanted his beloved to have a reminder of their years together in Arizona. And so he hired a flatbed truck, which hauled the 29,000-pound rock from Arizona that marks Bombeck's grave.

||||||||||||||||||||||||||||||||||||||||||||||||||||||||||||||||||||||||||||||||||||||||||||||||||||||||||||||||||

Novel Ways to Cap Off a Career

A cat on a hot tin roof can do a better balancing act than playwright Tennessee Williams (1911–1983) was able to manage on February 24, the day he choked on a medicine bottle cap in his room at New York's Hotel Elysee. The autopsy report determined that the cap "of the type used on nasal spray or eye solution" was accidently "swallowed or inhaled." Holding the cap between his teeth was a regular habit; that day his actions may have been blurred by all the secobarbital and alcohol found in his system. Williams's body was interred in Calvary Cemetery in St. Louis, Missouri, despite the fact that he made it known he wanted to be buried at sea ("12 hours north of Havana") at approximately the same spot in the Gulf of Mexico where Hart Crane, the poet and writer whom Williams considered one of his most significant influences, jumped to his death.

* * *

SOME men can't hold their liquor. Just ask Sherwood Anderson (1876–1941), who couldn't hold onto life after he accidentally swallowed a piece of a toothpick that was in a martini olive. The embedded toothpick caused the author to develop peritonitis. While on a goodwill tour to South America, he fell sick and died, on March 8 at age sixty-four, in Christobal, Canal Zone, Panama. He's buried at Round Hill Cemetery in Virginia. His cone-shaped gravestone reads "Life, Not Death, is the Great Adventure." Those who wish to learn even more about Sherwood can tour Ripshin Farm, his home in Troutdale, Virginia, which was declared a National Historic Landmark in 1971. Martinis will not be served.

AT 8:20 on the evening of August 11, as Margaret Mitchell (1900–1949) and her husband, John Marsh, were crossing Atlanta's Peachtree Street at 13th Street on their way to see the film *A Canterbury Tale*, the *Gone with the Wind* author was hit by a car going twice the posted speed limit of twenty-five miles an hour. Her unharmed husband held onto her as blood poured out of her left ear. Mitchell—who always feared she'd die from a car crash—was rushed to Grady Hospital where she spent the next five days. She never regained consciousness, though hospital reports recall that "at infrequent intervals, she had murmured vague, incoherent responses to spoken questions." (Witnesses claimed that Mitchell stepped into the street without looking, an action her friends said was habitual.)

On August 16, at 11:59 in the morning, Mitchell, forty-nine, was finally gone with the wind. X-rays revealed her skull was fractured from the top of her head to the top of the spine and that her pelvis was fractured in two places. Wearing a gown pinned with two orchids, Mitchell was buried in a silver-colored casket topped with a sheet of heavy glass.

Shortly after Mitchell died, Hugh D. Gravitt, twenty-nine, surrendered voluntarily to police. The off-duty taxi driver was driving his personal automobile; at the time of the accident, he had been out on bond of $5,450 for twenty-three previous traffic violations. Before beginning his sentence, he ran his car into a truck, injuring himself and his wife. Gravitt was convicted of involuntary manslaughter and served eleven months in prison.

SOME people do find the humor in death. When famed poet, writer, and founding member of the Algonquin Hotel's Round Table Dorothy Parker (1893–1967) learned that her husband and writing partner Alan Campbell (1904–1963) had died, a neighbor asked, "Dottie dear. What can I do to help you?" Dorothy shot back, "Get me a new husband." When the neighbor expressed her shock at such a distasteful remark, Dottie replied, "Sorry. Then run to the corner and get me a ham and cheese on rye and tell them to hold the mayo."

It gets funnier. Or sadder, depending on your take. When Dorothy died of a heart attack, her body was cremated two days later in New York. (Once asked to write her own epitaph, the woman who four times failed at suicide quipped "Excuse My Dust.") Parker had no heirs, so she left her literary estate to Dr. Martin Luther King Jr. whom she had never met. Within a year of her death, Dr. King was assassinated and the Parker estate rights reverted to the National Association for the Advancement of Colored People, which, to this day, benefits from the royalties from all Parker publications and productions.

Parker named fellow author Lillian Hellman as her executor. Hellman made all the funeral arrangements (even though Parker didn't want one) except for one thing: She didn't tell the crematory what to do with Dorothy's ashes. They sat on a shelf in the crematorium for six years until, on July 16, 1973, they were mailed to Parker's Wall Street attorney Paul O'Dwyer. He didn't know what to do with them, so he tucked them away for fifteen years in a filing cabinet. In 1988, Dorothy was finally parked for good. Twenty-one years after her death, with New York newspapers screaming torrid headlines over the mess, the NAACP built a memorial garden at its national headquarters in Baltimore and interred the ashes there under a brown brick circular memorial meant to symbolize the Round Table.

||||||||||||||||||||||||||||||||||||||||||||||||||||||||||||||||||||||||||||||||||||||||||||||||||||||||||||||||||

The three longest obituaries to run in the *New York Times*:

In first place: Pope John Paul II (1920–2005), 13,870 words, followed by Richard Nixon (1913–1994) at 13,155 words, and Ronald Reagan (1911–2004) at 11,411 words.   ☻

||||||||||||||||||||||||||||||||||||||||||||||||||||||||||||||||||||||||||||||||||||||||||||||||||||||||||||||||||

ASHES to ashes, dust to dust. Maybe. When esteemed English author, poet, and playwright David Herbert Richards Lawrence (1885–1930) died of tuberculosis, he was buried in a local cemetery, but at the request of his wife, Frieda, his body was exhumed five years later. Now here is where the story gets as convoluted as some of Lawrence's prose. D.H.'s remains were cremated, and Angelo Ravagli, Frieda's lover and the man entrusted with the task of taking Lawrence's ashes on a boat to America, later admitted that he tossed the ashes overboard. When Ravagli disembarked in New York, he put found ashes in an urn; it's supposedly those ashes that, on September 11, 1935, were mixed into concrete and poured into a slab that's the center point of the D. H. Lawrence shrine set in a small chapel at Kiowa

Ranch outside of Taos, New Mexico. Frieda died of a heart attack on her birthday in 1956. She's also buried at the shrine, but in an outside grave since she didn't want to intrude on her former hubby.

Not Going So Gently into the Night

NO one could ever accuse poet Sara Teasdale (1884–1933) of being a tease. Divorced, sickly, and miserably unhappy, she did what any stereotypically unhappy poet would do: wrote a suicide note, took an overdose of sleeping pills, lay down in a warm bath, fell asleep, and made obit history. Her final book of poetry was published that year.

AUTHOR William Faulkner called Thomas Clayton Wolfe (1900–1938) his generation's "best writer"—pretty heady stuff. When Wolfe died of tuberculosis of the brain, his coffin was too small to accommodate his six-foot, seven-inch body. A call was put out to a New York casket maker for a specially sized one, and today, Wolfe rests in it in Riverside Cemetery in Asheville, North Carolina, wearing a toupee to cover the incisions doctors made when they investigated his illnesses.

THE body of playwright Anton Chekhov (1860–1904) was returned to Moscow for his funeral in a refrigerated railcar carrying fresh oysters. Chekhov had been at a German spa, where he sought treatment for his worsening tuberculosis, when he died. His casket, thought by unknowing German train officials to be "perishable cargo," was placed on top of the ice-filled bushels.

IF only famed poet Dante Gabriel Rossetti had thought before he acted. After his depressed wife, Elizabeth Eleanor Siddal (1829–1862), killed herself, the famed poet placed a copy of his poems—the only copy—in her flowing red hair before she was buried.

And then one day Rossetti was in a poetry mode and needed his works back.

So, in 1869, Rossetti and his agent were given permission to have Elizabeth exhumed—the body was dug out late at night, the better to avoid scandal. The book of poetry was there, though a worm had burrowed through the pages.

Going Down in History

ROYALS, REGULAR JOES, AND MESSY MYTHS

Reports of My Death Have Been Greatly Exaggerated

GOOD news and bad news: The twain shall meet. On June 2, 1897, while on tour in Europe, humorist Mark Twain (1835–1910) was shocked to read his own obituary in the paper. Yet he was still able to find humor in such a situation, immediately shooting off a telegram to the Associated Press: THE REPORT OF MY DEATH WAS AN EXAGGERATION.

Twain seemed to be able to predict the future. In 1909, he said, "I came in with Halley's Comet in 1835. It is coming again next year, and I expect to go out with it. It will be the greatest disappointment of my life if I don't go out with Halley's Comet. The Almighty has said, no doubt: 'Now here are these two unaccountable freaks; they came in together, they must go out together.'"

His prediction was right: Twain died of heart attack on April 21 in Redding, Connecticut, one day after the comet's closest approach to Earth. His body was shipped to his wife's hometown of Elmira, New York, where the family maintained a summer home. Twain is buried in his wife's family plot at Woodlawn Cemetery.

||||||||||||||||||||||||||||||||||||||||||||||||||||||||||||||||||||||||||||||||||||||||||||||||||||||||||||||||||||||||||||||

So much for typesetters. When famed naturalist and ornithologist John James Audubon (1785–1851) died, his obituary listed his name as "Anderson." That's most likely the reason so few people turned out for the funeral. ☻

||||||||||||||||||||||||||||||||||||||||||||||||||||||||||||||||||||||||||||||||||||||||||||||||||||||||||||||||||||||||||||||

THE premature obituary of Alfred Nobel (1833–1896) condemned the Swedish scientist for his invention of dynamite. The obituary stated "the merchant of death is dead—Dr. Alfred Nobel, who became rich by finding ways to kill more people faster than ever before, died yesterday." Years later, Nobel's last will and testament set aside the bulk of his estate to establish the Nobel Prize, which rewards significant achievements in Physics, Chemistry, Physiology or Medicine, Literature, and notably, Peace—a way to make peace with what he had read.

No-Brainers
(and Other Personal Losses)

AND you thought you were smart. Not as smart (or dumb for that matter) as Thomas Stoltz Harvey, the pathologist who performed the autopsy on Albert Einstein (1879–1955), removing his brain within seven hours of the scientist's death at age seventy-six, on April 18, of a burst aortic aneurysm. Harvey, who removed the organ without consent, claimed he hoped that studying the brain tissues would reveal useful information about how and why Albert was such a smart guy. Harvey injected the 2.7 pound brain with all sorts of stuff, photographed it from every conceivable angle, then dissected it into 240 sections. He also removed Einstein's eyes, giving them as a present to Einstein's eye doctor Henry Abrams. Einstein's orbs are safely tucked away in an anonymous New York City bank vault and may, one day, end up on eBay. The rest of Einstein was cremated and his ashes scattered. No wonder Harvey was eventually fired from Princeton Hospital after refusing to give back the organs. In 1978, Albert's brain was discovered by a journalist working on a story; it again was in the hands of Harvey. Actually, it wasn't in his hands, but preserved in formaldehyde in two large Mason jars, in a cider box under a beer cooler, at his house.

The result of such a no-brainer? Einstein's brain was larger than most people's, proving that yes, size does matter. In 1998, Harvey was tired of caring for the brain, and donated it to the pathology department at the University Medical Center at Princeton. No one knows or cares about what happened to Harvey and his brain, though he did have some balls.

THERE'S a chill in the air. That's because when he died of cancer at seventy-three, retired psychology professor James H. Bedford (1893–1967) became the first human being to be cryonically preserved. His will left $4,200 for a steel capsule and liquid nitrogen to keep his body frozen at about 200 degrees below zero centigrade. When Bedford died on January 12, his doctor and a member of the Cryonics Society of California packed the body in ice. Eight hours later, Bedford was frozen solid. Artificial respiration and external heart massage protected the brain from oxygen-loss damage; Bedford's blood was replaced with antifreeze. Then the human-icle was flown to Phoenix where it was placed in liquid nitrogen storage. Note to Viagra users: This is not what's known as being stiff.

* * *

EVEN those high up on the Eucharist chain can be conned. Witness Pope Pius XII (1876–1958), who was duped by Riccardo Galeazzi-Lisi, a charlatan who posed as a medical doctor. His "treatments" for the ailing pontiff involved encasing the Pope in a cellophane bag into which Galeazzi-Lisi inserted aromatic herbs, spices, oils, and resins. He swore (on the Bible?) the Pope would be free of contamination for at least a hundred years.

Instead, the treatments gave the Holy Daddy rotting teeth and chronic hiccups. When the Pope went to meet his maker, Mr. Con Man embalmed the body so badly the corpse rapidly rotted and turned purple—and then his nose fell off. But as the body lay in state on a raised bier, the high temperature in St. Peter's caused a chemical reaction and Galeazzi-Lisi was forced to repeat the embalming procedure twice. The smell was so bad . . . well, thank God the Pope didn't have a nose.

For such a great baseball player, Ty Cobb (1886–1961) struck out when he died: Only three old baseball players attended his funeral, viewing his body through a glass-topped bronze casket.

AND we thought we were pack rats. John K. Lattimer (1914–2007) has us beat. When the prominent urologist (his patients included Greta Garbo, Katharine Hepburn, and Charles Lindbergh) died, it was discovered he had quite the collection. Lattimer owned the blood-stained collar of President Lincoln's coat and Hermann Göring's cyanide canister. But most importantly, he owned the penis of Napoleon Bonaparte (1769–1821). Napoleon died in exile on the remote island of Saint Helena on May 5; the next day an autopsy was done in the presence of seventeen witnesses. One kept his heart (the little emperor had bequeathed it to Empress Marie-Louise but it was never delivered) and stomach (the better to study the cancer that supposedly killed him). Another witness claimed his phallus. In 1924 the lot of Napoleonic artifacts was sold to a Philadelphia bibliophile for $2,000. When the mummified member was put on display at the Museum of French Art in New York, one critic wrote the penis looked "like a maltreated strip of buckskin shoelace or shriveled eel." Others called it "a shriveled sea horse," "a small shriveled finger," and (our fave), "one inch long and resembling a grape." Lattimer eventually purchased the boner for $3,000. The doctor had the "grape" X-rayed to confirm that it was indeed a human penis and asked the French government to provide a sample of Napoleon's DNA for comparison. They said no, not oui! oui! His daughter Evan inherited the collection after his death; she refused an offer of $100,000 for the Napoleonic phallus. The private remains her private affair.

WE hate to paint such a bleak picture, but one of the world's most revered painters, Rembrandt Harmenszoon van Rijn (1606–1669), is nowhere to be found. He died in poverty on October 4, and was buried four days later at Amsterdam's Westerkerk in an unmarked grave along the northern wall. Rembrandt's housekeeper and lover Hendrickje Stoffels (1626–1663) is also buried here, and his son Titus van Rijn (1641–1668) may also be. When the Protestant church's heating system was replaced, his grave (and those of many others) was removed and relocated to the north wall. Just one slight problem: No one is exactly sure which remains are Rembrandt's, and his body has never been identified. That didn't stop artful aficionados from commemorating his last-known resting spot, as well as his three hundredth birthday, with a stone marker that was erected in 1906. Call it a tombstone; we prefer a brush with greatness.

AFTER explorer Sir Walter Raleigh (1552–1618) was beheaded at the Tower of London for treason, his embalmed head was presented to his wife Elizabeth before his body was buried. Liz kept the head in a red velvet bag for the last twenty-nine years of her life. When she croaked, the head was cared for by their son before being reunited with Walter in his tomb in Westminster Abbey.

DEATH can be a pain. But not being properly buried is even worse. Revolutionary War patriot and agitator Thomas Paine (1737–1809) is remembered today for his pamphlet *Common Sense*, which advocated America's independence from Great Britain. By the time Paine died, he was scorned, broke, and a recluse. One obituary remarked, "he had lived long, did some good and much harm."

On June 8, he was buried on his farm in New Rochelle, New York. Only six people attended the burial, including the coffin maker seeking payment. Ten years later, Paine's grave was dug up by radical William Cobbett, whose intent was to take the remains to England, where Paine spent thirty-seven years, for reburial. It never happened. Instead, Cobbett kept Paine's remains in a trunk in the attic and upon his death, Cobbett's son auctioned off the bones. In 1987, a Sydney businessman claimed that he bought Paine's skull while on vacation in London. (He also claims he's a descendant of an illegitimate child of Paine's.) The fine folks at the now-defunct Thomas Paine National Historical Association in New Rochelle offer a heads-up, insisting they have Paine's petrified brain stem buried on the grounds of Thomas Paine Cottage, in a secret location. Ask the cottage keepers about the claim and they shrug it off, insisting the stem is in "storage" with other Historical Association artifacts.

TOO bad Tycho Brahe (1546–1601) isn't still around. He'd be perfect to star in one of those ubiquitous incontinence commercials. The famed Danish astronomer didn't make it to the men's room before a fancy (and long) banquet dinner began, so he held it . . . and held it . . . and held it. His manners were such that even thinking of leaving the room for a quick pee break was a no-no. He died eleven days later of an infection caused by a burst bladder. He was fifty-four. An interesting side note: Brahe's nose had been slashed off in a December 1566 duel and he wore a silver and copper prosthesis painted to match his skin tone. When his body was exhumed for reburial in 1901, the fake nose was missing—perhaps it had been stolen, perhaps time had rotted it. A green stain (from the copper) was in its place.

Saints, Sinners, and Royal Messes

SHE was one tough broad with one strong head on her shoulders. Just how strong was Mary Queen of Scots (1542–1587)? When Elizabeth I of England, so threatened by dear Mary, called for her beheading, it was something right out of a Fellini film. Mary was executed on February 8 at Fotheringhay Castle but it took two strokes of the ax to remove her head. The first blow missed her neck and struck the back of her head, at which point Queen Mary whispered, "Sweet Jesus." The second blow severed the neck except for a small bit of sinew that the executioner had to remove by "sawing" it off with the ax. When all was done, the executioner held Mary's head high in the air, crying, "God save the Queen!" But Mary got the last laugh: She had worn an auburn-colored wig to her date with death; the wig came off in the executioner's hand, while Mary's head (with her short silver hair) thumped to the ground.

VICIOUS barbarian dwarf Attila the Hun (406–453), the king and general of the Hun Empire, was one mean SOB. He wiped cities off the face of the earth and killed hundreds of thousands of people who got in his way. And just like his life, his death was shrouded in blood . . . lots of it. Attila was spending his honeymoon with his new bride Ildico. The next morning, he was found dead, drowned in his own blood. Everyone thought it was a nosebleed; indeed, much of the blood emerged from his nostrils, but he actually suffered from esophageal varices—a hemorrhoid in the lower part of his esophagus ruptured, forcing Attila to choke on his own blood.

As a tribute, his fellow Huns cut off their hair and slashed their flesh with their swords. Attila was buried in secret in a coffin made of gold, silver, and iron. Those who buried him were murdered so that the location would never be known.

PROOF that the French do know what they are doing: On February 16, French president Felix Faure (1841–1899) died from apoplexy right at the moment of orgasm—he was being serviced by his thirty-year-old mistress Marguerite Steinheil in the private quarters of the presidential palace. It wasn't long before she called for servants, who found the spent Felix lying on the couch while Marguerite adjusted her clothing.

SO much for peace and love. On January 20, while holding a prayer and pacification meeting in New Delhi, India, political and spiritual leader Mohandas Karamchand Gandhi

(1869–1948) was shot at point-blank range by Hindu fanatic Nathuram Godse. It was the sixth and final attempt to kill Gandhi. Like all great souls, Gandhi understood forgiveness, pardoning his assassin before losing consciousness and dying with his head in the lap of his sixteen-year-old niece.

Thousands watched Gandhi's sandalwood funeral pyre while sitting down to avoid being hurt by flying embers. Several urns were filled with Gandhi's ashes and milk taken from a sacred cow, and sent throughout India for memorial services. Most were buried at the Holy Triveni Sangam at Allahabad. One urn made its way to the Self-Realization Fellowship Lake Shrine in Pacific Palisades, California, the only U.S. site of Gandhi's ashes.

RUSSIAN tsar Peter the Great (1672–1725) didn't have a very good way with people. He had his eldest son, Alexei, tortured and killed because father and son didn't share the same political beliefs. To punish his half-sister Sophia for encouraging a political uprising, he banished her to a convent, then ordered three of the troublemaking military corps to be hanged directly outside the window of her room—the bodies were left hanging there for a year! When Peter learned that William Mons, the younger brother of his first mistress, became his wife Catherine's lover, Peter had him beheaded. He then stored the head in a jar, placing it in Catherine's bedroom as a reminder of the power (and pain) he could inflict.

He pissed them off, but he got his just due: Peter suffered from urinary tract and bladder problems; at one point, doctors were forced to perform surgery to release four pounds of blocked urine. He died early on the morning of February 8, 1725, from a gangrene-infected bladder.

||||||||||||||||||||||||||||||||||||||||||||||||||||||||||||||||||||||||||||||||||||||||||||||||||||||||||||||||||||||||||||||||

During the funeral of Alexander Graham Bell (1847–1922), telephone service throughout the United States and Canada was suspended for one minute, beginning at 6:25 p.m.   ☻

||||||||||||||||||||||||||||||||||||||||||||||||||||||||||||||||||||||||||||||||||||||||||||||||||||||||||||||||||||||||||||||||

Heil Hell!

EVIL does exist in human form. His name: Adolph Hitler (1889–1945). In April 1945, during the waning days of World War II and knowing Soviet troops were closing in and the end was near, Hitler moved into the Führerbunker, fifty feet below the Chancellery buildings in Berlin. The underground complex contained thirty rooms on two separate floors. Propaganda Minister Joseph Goebbels moved his entire family, including six young children, to live with Hitler in the bunker. On a daily basis, Hitler held meetings and chose which papers and documents were to be burned. On April 22, during a three-hour meeting, Hitler became hysterical, screaming denunciations of the army and raging like a madman at the "universal treason, corruption, lies, and failures" of those who had deserted him. The end had come; the Third Reich was a failure.

The mustached madman spent his last days drugged, but he was coherent enough to have a plan of action. He and longtime girlfriend, Eva Braun (1912–1945) whom he married a day before their deaths, would kill themselves at the right moment. Their actions were not desperate whims, but carefully planned final exit scenes. To make sure the cyanide capsules Hitler and Braun were planning to chew would work he had his handler give one to his dog, Blondi. (Hitler would then have the handler shoot the dog's five pups, including Hitler's favorite, Wolf.)

Hitler was a vegetarian; his last meal was spaghetti with a "light sauce." He chatted with Eva and staff about dog breeding and how lipstick was made. And then, at about 3:30 p.m. on April 30, he shot himself in the right temple at the same time he bit into a cyanide capsule. Eva simply bit.

Once discovered, their bodies were removed from their bombproof bunker, taken outdoors, put in a wooden bomb crate, doused with gasoline, set ablaze, and buried in a shallow grave. There was so much damage to the corpses that autopsies were not done, giving rise to the rumor that the bodies were not those of Hitler and Braun.

No one knew what happened to their remains after the fall of the Soviet Union. Archive records revealed that the bodies of Hitler and Eva Braun (along with Joseph and Magda Goebbels, the six Goebbels children, General Hans Krebs, and Hitler's beloved dogs Blondi and Daisy) were secretly buried in graves in East Germany. In 1970, then-KGB chief Yuri Andropov ordered the bones disinterred and incinerated. And so the German gang were dug up, cremated, and scattered in the Elbe River by the Soviets.

Well, not all of Hitler. According to the Russian Federal Security Service, KGB members rummaging through Hitler's bunker took fragments of his skull as souvenirs. Also in their archives: Hitler's lower jawbone, confirmed as authentic by Hitler's dental records.

Hitler wrote his last will and testament at 4 a.m. on the morning before his suicide. In part, it reads: "I have decided therefore to remain in Berlin and there of my own free will to choose death at the moment when I believe the position of the Fuehrer and Chancellor itself can no longer be held. I die with a joyful heart . . ."

‖‖‖

Princess Grace Kelly (1929–1982) was buried in a silk-lined coffin wearing a white gown and her wedding ring and clutching rosary beads. At her funeral service, Princess Diana and Nancy Reagan sat together.   ☻

‖‖‖

Misadventures and Mishaps

NO one could ever accuse English philosopher, statesman, and scientist (and the man who claimed he was the real Shakespeare) Sir Francis Bacon (1561–1626) of being chicken when it came to trying new things. On a drive through the snowy streets of London, it hit him that the cold white stuff might be used as a better food preservative than salt. So off he and his companion, who happened to be the king's doctor, went. They stopped at the house of a poultry saleswoman, bought a bird, and had the woman eviscerate it. Then Bacon proceeded to stuff the carcass with snow. And that's when he contracted pneumonia; even eating the frozen chicken failed to help. He died a couple of days later, chilled to the bone.

HARRY "The Horse" Flamburis (1940–1977), who was president of the Northern California Hells Angels in the mid-1970s, did not die in a pretty way: He and his girlfriend were found bound with duct tape and shot execution-style. He was buried in a double vault on April 22 in Cypress Lawn Cemetery outside of San Francisco; a couple of months later, a group of Flamburis's Angels friends took his Harley and buried it on top of him. When a reporter asked tour director Marilyn Calvey why the cemetery would allow such a move, she quipped, "Who is going to question 180 Hells Angels?" When Flamburis's dog Chopper finally passed on, he was buried at nearby Pet's Rest Cemetery in Colma, California— with a toy Harley-Davidson.

THE father of modern aircraft, Orville Wright, was also responsible for the first airplane fatality. It was September 17, and Wright was testing a new aircraft for the U.S. Army at Fort Myer, Virginia. Aviation expert Lt. Thomas E. Selfridge (1882–1908) was tagging along for the ride. The plane took off at 5:14 p.m.; after circling Fort Myer several times at 150 feet, the wood propeller snapped, sending the aircraft into a nosedive. Wright shut off the engine and tried to stabilize the craft, now hurling to the ground at a 45-degree angle. The plane crashed and both men were pinned beneath it. Wright suffered leg fractures, broken ribs, and an injured back, while Selfridge received a severe compound fracture at the base of his skull. He underwent immediate surgery but died three hours later without ever regaining consciousness. Selfridge was buried at Arlington National Cemetery, a mere hundred feet from where the plane crashed.

QUITE a number, that Jasper Newton "Jack" Daniel (1846 or 1850–1911). The bearded gent responsible for an alarming rate of alcoholism couldn't get the office safe opened one morning at his Lynchburg, Tennessee, distillery, so he kicked it. Hard. The kick caused infection to set into his toe, which turned into blood poisoning. (He should have just stuck the toe in a vat of whiskey.) Jack can be found at Lynchburg City Cemetery in Lynchburg, Tennessee. Chairs set up alongside his gravestone offer the chance for visitors to sit and drink in the sight.

Proof Why One "Auto" Always Carry Out Another's Final Wishes

WHEN Texas oil millionaire widow Sandra Ilene West (1939–1977) knew the end was near (she was planning to overdose), she gave explicit directions to her brother-in-law, Sol West. She was to be buried in her baby blue 1964 Ferrari 250GT, with the driver's seat "slanted at a comfortable angle," and she was to be wearing her favorite lace nightgown. She and the car were to be interred in a large wood, steel, and concrete box and covered over with two truckloads of cement to discourage vandals. She promised Sol a cool $2 mil if he carried out her wishes or a lousy $10,000 if he did not. He did. The funeral cost $17,000, and woman and car are resting in a nine-foot deep hole at Alamo Masonic Cemetery in San Antonio, Texas.

HOWARD Hughes (1905–1976) may have been one of the richest men in the world, but he was also as nutty as a fruitcake. The recluse died at 1:27 p.m., while en route from his penthouse in Freeport, Grand Bahama, to the Methodist Hospital in Houston. What officials saw shocked them: His drug use had made him practically unrecognizable. His hair, beard, fingernails, and toenails had grown absurdly long, and he had shrunk two inches from his six-foot, four-inch frame. He was so malnourished that he weighed only ninety pounds. The FBI had to use fingerprints to positively identify the body. And though Hughes's autopsy revealed he died of kidney failure, the billionaire was in such poor physical health that X-rays revealed broken-off hypodermic needles still embedded in his arms.

WE could, if we really wanted to stretch it, call the death of civil engineer John Augustus Roebling (1800–1869) muddled in troubled waters. The man most famous for designing the Brooklyn Bridge died because of that landmark. While he was looking for a site to build one of the bridge's towers, a ferry boat crashed into the pier on which he was standing. He didn't move fast enough, his foot was crushed, and he died, on July 22, from tetanus poisoning that had developed from the injury. Those wanting to visit his grave in Riverview Cemetery in Trenton, New Jersey, need to take the George Washington Bridge.

Forever Out of Tune

HITTING ALL THE WRONG NOTES

Tex-Mex Tragedy

SELENA Quintanilla-Perez (1971–1995), the singer Tom Brokaw once dubbed "the Mexican Madonna," was shot to death by Yolanda Saldivar, her former employee and her fan club president who had been embezzling money from the star. Selena decided to confront Saldivar in person, hoping to resolve the situation without resorting to legal action. She asked Saldivar to bring accounting paperwork, and they agreed to meet on March 30 in Room 158 of the Days Inn in Corpus Christi, Texas. Saldivar did not bring the paperwork (she stalled by claiming she had been raped in Mexico; Selena drove her to the hospital where doctors dismissed the charge when not finding evidence of rape) and began to argue with the singer. At 11:48 a.m., Saldivar pulled a gun out of her purse, pointing it to her own head before shooting Selena. The bullet struck the singer in her right shoulder, yet she was able to make it to the motel lobby, where she collapsed. Selena was rushed to the hospital—the same one she and her assassin were at earlier—where at 1:09 p.m. she was pronounced dead.

Her death stunned the Hispanic world. More than fifty thousand fans filed by Selena's casket; when she was laid to rest at Seaside Memorial Park on April 3—thirteen days before her twenty-fourth birthday—more than eight thousand white roses covered her grave.

Two weeks after her death, George W. Bush, then governor of Texas, declared her birthday "Selena Day" in Texas; in 1997, Warner Brothers made a film based on her life starring Jennifer Lopez. Selena was buried three years and a day after her wedding to guitarist Chris Perez. The Days Inn has since renumbered its rooms, yet knowing fans continue to leave flowers and gifts at the room's door. Selena's family opened a "condolence line" so die-hard fans could leave messages . . . at a cost of $3.99 per minute.

And then there's Howard Stern.

A few days after the murder, the shock jock mocked Selena and knocked her music: "Alvin and the Chipmunks have more soul," he said. His remarks outraged Selena's fans and Texas's Hispanic community, and a judge ordered a disorderly conduct arrest warrant. Stern later made an on-air apology—in Spanish.

Souvenir hunters take note: The .38-caliber revolver used to kill Selena was smashed with a sledgehammer and thrown into Corpus Christi Bay on orders of a state judge. Saldivar was convicted of murder and sentenced to life in prison, and will be eligible for parole in October 2025.

The Sounds of Silence

AT the funeral of her pal Louis Armstrong (1901–1971), songstress Peggy Lee (1920–-2002) was so distraught that she sang "The Lord's Prayer" so quietly planes flying in and out of nearby LaGuardia Airport drowned her out. At Westwood Memorial Park, where Lee is laid to rest, fans can actually sit on her body—her ashes are within a marble bench chiseled with the phrase "Music is my life's breath."

STILL crying over the death of singer Roy Orbison (1936–1988)? He was on tour with the Traveling Wilburys (which included former Beatle George Harrison) when he suffered a heart attack and died at his mother's house. Ironically, one of his last recordings was a version of his hit "Crying," sung as a duet with his good pal k.d. lang, and for which he won a Grammy. Let the crying continue: Orbison is still buried in an unmarked grave. Orbison's family had planned to install an elaborate, black granite headstone engraved with the titles of his hits, but grave No. 97 in Section D at Westwood Memorial Park remains unmarked.

TALK about a surprise party. Marvin Gaye (1939–1984) was shot to death by his father on April 1—no fooling—the day before he would have turned forty-five. At the time, Gaye's career had taken an upswing, and the IRS problems that forced him to flee America and live in Europe seemed to be under control. But Gaye's dependence on cocaine was not. He moved in with his parents, hoping to keep clean. Wrong move. Father and son never got along—sources say the senior Gaye abused Marvin as a child and resented his success. They argued so much that Marvin threatened to kill himself. He didn't have to. Marvin's mother witnessed the shooting: "I was standing about eight feet away from Marvin, when my husband came to the door of the bedroom with his pistol. My husband didn't say anything, he just pointed the gun at Marvin. I screamed but it was very quick. My husband shot and Marvin screamed. I tried to run. Marvin slid down to the floor after the first shot."

Daddy had good aim: The first bullet entered Marvin's chest at a 30-degree downward angle, perforating the right lung, heart, diaphragm, liver, stomach, and left kidney before coming to rest against his left flank. It was immediately fatal. Then Daddy fired again at point-blank range, before going outside, tossing the .38 caliber gun onto the lawn, sitting down, and waiting for the police. Daddy was charged with first-degree murder but the charges were dropped after doctors discovered he was suffering from a brain tumor.

THURSDAY, July 16, 1981: The night that made singer/songwriter Harry Chapin (1942–1981) infamous. It was a little past noon, and Chapin was driving his 1975 blue Volkswagen Rabbit on the Long Island Expressway at about sixty-five miles per hour. He was on his way to a concert; as he neared exit 40, Chapin knew he was having a heart attack. He slowed the car down, put on his emergency flashers, and veered into the center lane. He almost collided with another car, swerving left, then right again, ending up directly in front of a tractor trailer. The truck couldn't brake in time and rammed the rear of Chapin's car, sparks igniting the ruptured gas tank, which immediately burst into flames. The truck's driver and a passerby were able to extract Chapin from the burning Rabbit by cutting him out of his seat belt. He was taken by helicopter to Nassau County Medical Center where ten doctors spent thirty minutes trying to revive him. No luck. Chapin was dead of cardiac arrest.

Although Chapin was driving without a license (it was revoked because of numerable traffic violations) his widow Sandy Gaston won a $12 million decision in a negligence lawsuit against the owners of the truck.

IMAGINE all the people / Living life in peace. Now imagine John Lennon (1940–1980) and that peace is shattered by the four bullets crazed fan Mark David Chapman shot into the former Beatle's back (the fifth shot missed) as Lennon and his wife, Yoko Ono, returned home from a recording session. Chapman, thanks to a $2,500 loan from his credit union, arrived in New York where he had been stalking the forty-year-old Lennon for a few days; earlier on the night of the murder, he even had Lennon autograph a copy of *Double Fantasy*.

At 10:49 p.m., Lennon staggered to the apartment building's guard's office and cried, "I'm shot!" He was pronounced dead on arrival in the emergency room of Roosevelt Hospital at 11:15 p.m. The next day, the grieving widow and their son Sean issued a statement: "There is no funeral for John. John loved and prayed for the human race. Please pray the same for him. Love, Yoko and Sean."

Interestingly, about three weeks before his death, Lennon fired his bodyguards; anyone trying to kill him, he surmised, would first shoot the bodyguard. That's one theory that really didn't come together. Lennon was cremated two days after his murder. The location of his ashes are in dispute: Some believe they were scattered over Strawberry Fields, a three-and-a-half acre section of Central Park that was dedicated to John in April 1982, while others believe Ono still has them. In fact, Ono was so fearful that someone might steal her husband's remains that she had the ashes disguised as a Christmas present. Ono still lives at the Dakota; Chapman is still in prison, having been denied parole every time since the murder.

TUPAC Shakur (1971–1996), unlikely martyr of gangsta rap, may have died from "respiratory failure and cardiopulmonary arrest in connection with multiple gunshot wounds," but he was still smoking days after he was cremated—some of his ashes were later mixed with marijuana and smoked by members of his band.

Stairway to Heaven (or Is It Hell?)

WITH a name like Sid Vicious (1957–1979) what kind of demise do you expect? The punk rocking member of the Sex Pistols and his gal pal Nancy Spungen (1958–1978) had a violent, drug-induced relationship. On October 12, Nancy was found slumped over the toilet of Room 100 in Greenwich Village's Chelsea Hotel. She had been stabbed to death from a single wound to the abdomen—the knife was later traced to one owned by Vicious, who was arrested for murder. There's still speculation if he did it or not; the secret went to both of their graves. Sid confessed to the murder, but died before the trial ended, overdosing on some pure heroin his mother, Anne Beverley, bought him. Mother is rumored to have climbed a wall outside of King David Cemetery in Bensalem, Pennsylvania, and sprinkled Sid's ashes over Nancy's grave—the Spungen family refused to have the dead Sid anywhere near their dead daughter, plus the Jewish cemetery did not permit ash scattering. Still others believe Mama dropped the ashes at Heathrow Airport, and that Sid was sucked up by the ventilation system. Dust to dust?

IT was September 25, and Led Zeppelin drummer John Henry "Bonzo" Bonham (1948–1980) and assistant Rex King were on their way to rehearsals for an upcoming tour of the United States, the band's first since 1977. Bonham wanted to stop for breakfast—he downed two ham rolls and about sixteen shots of vodka. The drinking continued all day and into the night until the "sleeping" Bonham fell and was carried to bed at midnight. He was found dead hours later. The coroner's inquest revealed that in the twenty-four hours before he died, Bonham had drunk forty measures of vodka, which resulted in pulmonary edema—his lungs "waterlogged" as they filled with his vomit. The death was ruled accidental. Bonham was cremated and buried at Saint Michael's Church and Cemetery in Rushock, England. A cymbal sits in front of his headstone, unless it has been stolen by one of the groupies who leave behind drumsticks and booze bottles.

THE death of AC/DC lead singer Bon Scott (1946–1980) was deemed by the coroner as "death by misadventure"—Scott's stomach held the equivalent of a half bottle of whiskey and he choked to death on his own vomit.

WHEN singer/songwriter Gram Parsons (1946–1973) died on September 19, at twenty-six, from a combination of morphine and alcohol, his road manager Phil Kaufman and a friend Michael Martin did everything they could to carry out his final wish—to be cremated at Joshua Tree National Park and his ashes spread over the formation known as Cap Rock. So off they went to Los Angeles International Airport in a borrowed hearse, convincing authorities to hand over the corpse.

The pals then drove Parsons to Joshua Tree, where they poured five gallons of gasoline into his open coffin and threw in a lit match. Instant cremation? No—instead an instant fireball mutilated about 60 percent of the corpse. Like a scene out of a Keystone Kops comedy, the police gave chase. Gram's friends were eventually arrested several days later and fined around $700 for stealing a coffin (it was not against the law to steal a dead body). What was left of Gram was sent to his stepfather, who interred the charred remains in Garden of Memories in Metairie, Louisiana.

IIIIIIIIIIIIIIIIIIIIIIIIIIIIIIIIIIIIIIIIIIIIIIIIIIIIIIIIIIIIIIIIIIIIIIIIIIIIIIIIIIIIIIIIIIIIIIIIIIIIIIIIIIIIIIIIIIII

One of Tina Turner's pet dogs is buried in Pet's Rest in Colma, California, wrapped in one of her fur coats. 💀

IIIIIIIIIIIIIIIIIIIIIIIIIIIIIIIIIIIIIIIIIIIIIIIIIIIIIIIIIIIIIIIIIIIIIIIIIIIIIIIIIIIIIIIIIIIIIIIIIIIIIIIIIIIIIIIIIIII

* * *

JIM Morrison (1943–1971), Janis Joplin (1943–1970), and Jimi Hendrix (1942–1970) all died at twenty-seven of drug-induced deaths. (Jimi's official cause was a bit more descriptive: "inhalation of vomit due to barbiturate intoxication.") Joplin made changes to her will just two days before her death, setting aside $2,500 to pay for a posthumous all-night party for two hundred guests at her favorite pub "so my friends can get blasted after I'm gone." The Grateful Dead performed; the invitations read "Drinks are on Pearl!"

||||||||||||||||||||||||||||||||||||||||||||||||||||||||||||||||||||||||||||||||||||||||||||||||||||||||||||||||||||||||||||||

Rolling Stone guitarist Keith Richards admits snorting lots of substances in his life, but the strangest? Let him answer: "I snorted my father. He was cremated, and I couldn't resist grinding him up with a little bit of blow. My dad wouldn't have cared. It went down pretty well, and I'm still alive." What some people will do for a little satisfaction. No word as to whether Keith snorted some of mom, Doris, who died in 2007.   💀

||||||||||||||||||||||||||||||||||||||||||||||||||||||||||||||||||||||||||||||||||||||||||||||||||||||||||||||||||||||||||||||

IT would be easy to say that when Freddie Mercury (1946–1991), the leader of the British rock group Queen, died of AIDS, another one bit the dust. So we'll say it. And we'll add this: Before he died, he told his former girlfriend that she must never, ever tell anyone where his ashes are. His exact words, she recalled, were: "I don't want anyone to dig me up." Some ashes were scattered on the shore of Lake Geneva, Switzerland, near a statue of the singer. One of Mercury's last tunes was "Too Much Love Will Kill You." No, but too much unprotected sex might.

HIS was a most shocking demise, but, hey, at least Keith Relf (1943–1976) went out with a jolt of music. The lead singer and harmonica player of the Yardbirds was just thirty-three when he was electrocuted at his home studio in Hounslow, England—the electric guitar he was playing was not properly grounded. Talk about an electrifying performance.

KEVIN Michael "GG" Allin (1956–1993) gave punk music an extreme makeover. During live performances he would vomit, urinate, and defecate on the stage, taking laxatives at just the right time. He'd then eat the feces and fling them at the audience and somehow, in the midst of the mess, find a strung out groupie to give him oral sex. He even vowed he would kill himself onstage—he failed to keep that promise. Allin died of a heroin overdose at pal Johnny Puke's apartment. His brother refused to allow the mortician to bathe the body, and pals posed with the corpse. The thirty-six-year-old singer was buried in a black leather jacket and a jock strap, one hand holding a bottle of Jim Beam.

||||||||||||||||||||||||||||||||||||||||||||||||||||||||||||||||||||||||||||||||||||||||||||||||||||||||||||||||||||||||||

FRANK SINATRA (1915–1998)

Final resting place: Desert Memorial Park, Cathedral City, California

Ol' Blue Eyes died of a heart attack at 10:50 p.m. on May 14 at Cedars-Sinai Medical Center, with his fifth and final wife, Barbara, by his side. As attempts were made to stabilize him, Frank muttered "I'm losing"—hardly the lyric to a hit song, but nevertheless his final words.

Sinatra was laid to rest following a star-studded memorial service ceremony. Sharing his casket: a small bottle of Jack Daniel's, a pack of Camels, a Zippo lighter, a roll of cherry Life Savers, a few Tootsie Rolls, some stuffed animals, and, from daughter Tina, a dog biscuit ("for Dad's love of critters"), an envelope containing ten dimes, and a note that read "Sleep warm, Poppa—look for me." She knew Dad always needed change to make a phone call.   💀

You Can't Spell "Diet" Without "Die"

SHE is finally on top of the world, looking down on creation. Accomplished drummer Karen Carpenter (1950–1983), the female half of the best-selling duo the Carpenters, eventually lost her battle with anorexia nervosa. Her illness publicly surfaced in 1975, when the duo was forced to cancel a European tour because Karen was too weak to perform. She sought help, but never fully recovered; in 1982 she collapsed after a recording session and spent most of that year in treatment.

Brother Richard recalls that despite her problems, Karen was determined to recover and forge on. The recipe called for a new album and a weight gain. She had gained thirty pounds over a two-month stay in New York, but the sudden poundage, much of which was the result of intravenous feeding, further strained her heart, already stretched to the limit from years of crash dieting. It was later revealed that Karen was taking ten times the normal daily dose of thyroid replacement medication in order to speed up her metabolism, supplementing her weight-loss "plan" with heavy doses of laxatives.

On February 4, Karen went to her parents' home to sort through some old clothes. She and mom went to Bob's Big

Boy for lunch where Karen gulped down a heaping salad. She even took some tacos home. Early the next morning, her mother heard her stirring, and heard a bedroom closet door open. She found Karen on the floor of the closet. She was rushed to Downey Community Hospital, where she was pronounced dead twenty minutes later. She had suffered cardiac arrest at 9:51 a.m. Less than a month from her thirty-third birthday, Karen Carpenter was dead of "heartbeat irregularities brought on by chemical imbalances associated with anorexia nervosa." Richard denied published reports that Karen abused ipecac syrup, an over-the-counter emetic medicine that is only meant to be taken by persons who have accidentally swallowed poison, insisting that vomiting the syrup would damage her vocal cords.

Wearing a rose-colored suit, Karen lay in an open white casket. More than one thousand mourners filed past to say goodbye to love, among them friends Dorothy Hamill, Olivia Newton-John, Petula Clark, and Dionne Warwick. Carpenter's estranged husband Tom attended her funeral, took off his wedding ring, and threw it into the casket. (Ironically, their divorce was scheduled to be finalized on the day Karen died.) Originally interred in Forest Lawn Cypress, Karen's remains were moved to a stunning 46,000-pound crypt in the Tranquility Gardens section of Pierce Brothers Valley Oaks Memorial Park in late 2003. The epitaph says it all: "A Star on Earth, A Star in Heaven."

PERHAPS Tommy Dorsey (1905–1956) was thinking of the title of one of his hits, "This Is No Dream," in the final moments before his heart stopped cranking. The legendary musician and Big Band icon died at fifty-one in his Greenwich, Connecticut, home, choking in his sleep after a heavy meal. The food had lodged in his windpipe . . . the sleeping pills he had taken right after the meal may also have had something to do with it. Dorsey is buried in Kensico Cemetery in Valhalla, New York. His gravestone is decorated with a trombone and bar of music.

ON May 31, Billie Holiday (1915–1959) was in New York's Metropolitan Hospital suffering from liver and heart disease. Police officers were stationed at the door to her room since she had been arrested for heroin possession as she lay dying. When she finally expired on July 17, the cops were still there. Lady Day died with seventy cents in the bank and $750 in fifty-dollar bills strapped to her leg—the advance payment she received for an upcoming autobiography.

WHILE singing his hit "Lonely Teardrops" at a New Jersey concert on September 25, 1975, R&B giant Jackie Wilson (1934–1984) suffered a massive heart attack. He fell so hard headfirst onto the stage that he was left in a vegetative state until his death, at forty-nine, nearly a decade later. *American Bandstand* idol Dick Clark, who had sponsored the concert, paid all of Jackie's medical bills; but when Jackie died, the money stopped and Wilson was buried in an unmarked pauper's grave. In 1990, fans had his body exhumed and gave Wilson a proper burial in Westlawn Cemetery in Wayne, Michigan. His gravestone promises "No More Lonely Teardrops."

Diva Death

KATE Smith (1907–1986) was one show-biz heavyweight, tipping the scales at 235 pounds by the age of thirty. Such weighty issues didn't matter to the woman who never took a formal music lesson and whose recording of "God Bless America" is still played at many baseball games. "I'm big, and I sing, and boy, when I sing, I sing all over!" she once said.

When she died of diabetes, her demands were also big.

Almost too big. She refused to be buried in the ground; her will specifically requested she be interred "in a hermetically sealed bronze casket in a mausoleum sufficient to contain my remains alone." But cemetery bylaws banned above-ground burial spots, so Katie's hefty body was put in cold storage until the executors of her will and church officials hashed it out. On November 14, 1987, more than a year after her death, Smith was finally laid to permanent rest in a 6-foot, 8-inch high; 10-foot, 3-inch long; and 8-foot, 10¼ inch-wide mausoleum made of pink granite—with a back door—in St. Agnes Cemetery in Lake Placid, New York. Hers was the first, and remains the only, aboveground mausoleum in the cemetery.

||||||||||||||||||||||||||||||||||||||||||||||||||||||||||||||||||||||||||||||||||||||||||||||||||||||||||||||||||||||||||||

SALVATORE PHILLIP "SONNY" BONO (1935–1998)

Final resting place: Desert Memorial Park, Cathedral City, California

On January 5, the sixty-two-year-old was killed when he slammed headfirst, while skiing at close to thirty miles an hour, into a forty-foot pine tree. He died about 2 p.m., five hours before his frozen body was found off a trail in South Lake Tahoe. Autopsy reports claimed that there wasn't any indication of any substances or alcohol, but you better sit down, kids—Bono's widow, Mary, disagreed. Several months after her husband's death, Mary revealed that Sonny was a prescription drug abuser, taking "15, 20 maybe" pills a day at the time of his death. The pills were prescribed by doctors for chronic back and neck problems, and she is "100 percent convinced that is why he died. What he did showed absolute lack of judgment. That's what these pills do. They take away your thought process."

At the time of his death, Bono, a former mayor of Palm Springs, California, served as congressman from the State of California. Mary now holds that seat. Sonny's funeral on January 9 was broadcast live and flags flown at half-mast. Cher openly wept as she delivered the eulogy, calling her former husband and singing partner "the most unforgettable character I've ever met."   💀

||||||||||||||||||||||||||||||||||||||||||||||||||||||||||||||||||||||||||||||||||||||||||||||||||||||||||||||||||||||

ACTRESS and singer Alice Faye (1915–1998) died from stomach cancer at the age of eighty-three, but the news she took to her grave was (almost) too much to stomach. One of the last things she wanted to add to her resume was posing for one of those legendary "What Becomes a Legend Most?" ads for Blackglama furs. But it didn't happen. "I asked Rex Reed to find out why, and he came back and told me Blackglama didn't think I was a legend," she recalled. "If Diana Ross and Bette Midler are legends, what does that make me?"

Frankly, dead. Faye's ashes rest next to those of her hubby, singer and orchestra leader Phil Harris, in a glass case at Forest Lawn Cemetery in Cathedral City, California. His ashes are in a fancy urn decorated with leaping dolphins; hers are in an urn whose angel looks toward Heaven.

FRANK Sinatra said she was "the greatest entertainer who ever lived." But the death of Judy Garland (1922–1969) was a performance that could hardly be called entertaining.

Let's go back to London, June 1969 . . .

Judy, looking gaunt and sick and with a mouthful of rotten teeth, had married her fifth husband, nightclub owner and hanger-on Mickey Deans, a mere three months earlier. He was certain he could resurrect his wife's career, which was, at this point, as dead as she would soon be.

On the morning of June 22, Deans woke up to an empty bed. He called for his wife. The bathroom door was locked. He banged again and again. No answer. Deans climbed onto the roof of their flat and peered in the open window. There was Dorothy Gale, Mrs. Norman Maine, Frances Gumm, dead, at forty-seven, her arms on her lap; her head slumped forward, on the toilet. Deans crawled through the window. Judy's skin had turned blue, and blood was gushing from her nose and mouth. A comeback was certainly out of the picture. Judy had died sometime between 3 and 4:30 in the morning. She was so malnourished and dehydrated that when the medical examiner arrived, he "folded" Judy's body over his arm, as if she was a soiled piece of clothing, so that photographers wouldn't be able to snap her in such a sorry state. And though everyone wanted to believe it was suicide, the official autopsy reported stated she died from "an incautious overdose of barbiturates."

More than twenty-two thousand flocked past Judy's glass-topped steel casket (spray-painted blue), many of them gay men who stood in line for hours for a final glimpse of their idol. (Some actually carried portable record players, spinning vinyl so Judy's voice filled the air.) She wore blue eye shadow, orange lipstick, the silver lame gown in which she wed Deans, and a single strand of pearls. A prayer book was in her hands.

Garland, who died owing millions, was tucked in a temporary vault at Ferncliff Mausoleum in New York until someone could come up with the money to bury her. Finally, on November 4, 1970, more than a year after Judy went over the rainbow, she was laid to rest in a rather unattractive tan-flecked marble crypt. Daughter Liza Minnelli paid the expenses.

Gone Too Soon, Like a Comet Blazing 'Cross the Evening Sky

IMELDA Marcos cried when she heard the news. So did Madonna and Britney Spears and Berry Gordy and Tina Turner and Liza Minnelli and Smokey Robinson and Diana Ross and Elizabeth Taylor and Donna Summer and Usher and Celine Dion and Cher and about 16 zillion other fans of Michael Jackson (1958–2009). The report that the King of Pop had died of "massive cardiac arrest" at the age of fifty was really bad news. Other bad news that same day: Farrah Fawcett (1947–2009), the sixty-two-year-old baby boomer pinup girl and one-third of *Charlie's Angels*, died from anal cancer at 9:28 a.m.—a few hours before the death of Jackson. And yes, even in his death, Jackson stole the TV spotlight.

He may have likened himself to Peter Pan, but he lived in chaos, and his narcissistic flights of fancy—extravagant shopping sprees, so much plastic surgery that he ended up looking like the walking corpse of a singer formerly known as Miss Ross, dangling his infant son over a hotel balcony in Berlin while a throng of fans watched from below, his uncompromising obsession with fame, not eating properly because he wanted "a dancer's body," sleeping in a hyperbaric chamber that he swore would allow him to live to 150—sent him to the land of never. And we don't mean Neverland Ranch, which he lost when it went into foreclosure. (Jackson, who sold more than 750 million albums in his lifetime, died more than $500 million in debt.) You have to know something's not right with someone who insists white and red wine are okay to share with young boys since they are "Jesus Juice" and "Jesus' Blood."

At a little past midnight on the morning of June 25, Jackson arrived at the gated Holmby Hills mansion he was renting for $100,000 a month. He had been rehearsing for at least six hours a day for his upcoming fifty concerts in London—an effort to revive his career after several setbacks in the past decade; helping him get in shape was Lou "The Incredible Hulk" Ferrigno.

Later that day came the now-infamous 911 call. The Jackson staff member sounded urgent, reporting that though the singer's personal doctor was relentlessly "pumping his chest," Jackson was "not responding to anything." Paramedics for the L.A. Fire Department arrived at 12:21 p.m., rushing the singer to UCLA Medical Center, only a few minutes' drive away. Jackson was brain-dead when he arrived at the hospital. His parents had him removed from life support (his three children were at his bedside as well as his mom, dad, and siblings). The singer was officially pronounced dead at 2:26 p.m., though he was already dead by the time the paramedics arrived, despite some forty-two minutes of nonstop CPR. Fans were glued to the TV as the lifeless Jackson, wrapped in a white body bag, was transferred from the helicopter to the coroner's van. (If you watch closely, the body gets bumped . . . undoubtedly, Jackson's last attempt at making the right moves.)

Within hours of his death, someone was shrewd enough to make and sell (at $20 a pop) commemorative T-shirts while former family attorney Brian Oxman told anyone who would listen that he would not "keep quiet" about what he knew. What Oxman knew was known by many: Jackson was addicted to prescription painkillers. "I warned the family that Michael would one day wake up dead," he told every TV camera in sight. Noted spiritual leader Deepak Chopra recalled that when Jackson stayed with him for a week in 2005, the singer asked him for a prescription for OxyContin. Chopra refused, and Jackson stopped speaking to him. During the 2003 trial when Jackson was indicted for molesting a young cancer patient (he was acquitted on all charges), Jackson demonstrated erratic behavior—jumping onto an SUV and dancing and showing up for court in his pajama bottoms. One reporter who covered the trial said Jackson was so "extremely medicated" that he looked "like a zombie." Another called him "preserved in medication." This was the beginning of his end, though many insist that he first became addicted to painkillers in 1984, when Jackson's hair caught on fire during the filming of a Pepsi commercial.

Once the pixie dust had settled and the impromptu memorial vigils ended, what emerged was as unsettling as Jackson's skin color. Since the early 1990s, he had traveled with a personal physician, who gave him daily injections of drugs; the drugs helped numb the pain from what one insider calls "massive amounts of skin grafting." In 2007, he was sued by an L.A. pharmacy for owing $101,926 for prescription medication dating back to 2005. Lisa Marie Presley, to whom Jackson was married for two years, admitted that she often witnessed his weird side. "In trying to save him, I almost lost myself. I became very ill and emotionally, spiritually exhausted in my quest to save him from certain self-destructive behavior," she wrote on her blog. She also admitted that her former hubby once questioned her about the death of her father, Elvis Presley: "Years ago Michael and I were having a deep conversation about life in general. He stared at me very intensely and he stated with an almost calm certainty, 'I am afraid that I am going to end up like him, the way he did.' I promptly tried to deter him from the idea, at which point he just shrugged his shoulders and nodded almost matter of fact as if to let me know, he knew what he knew and that was kind of that."

He may have had fame and fortune, notoriety and new noses, but death? He couldn't beat it.

Food for Thought

CALORIES, CRAVINGS, AND CANNIBALISM

And You Thought *You* Should Call Jenny Craig

KING Adolf Frederick of Sweden (1710–1771) was considered a weak ruler but a very big eater. Make that BIG. After consuming a meal of lobster, sauerkraut, caviar, champagne, kippers, and fourteen servings of his favorite pastry served in hot milk, he developed such digestion problems that he died. Even Pepcid couldn't soothe this stomach. Swedish school children are (unofficially) taught that the king, who died on February 12, is "the king who ate himself to death," even thought the real cause was a stroke brought on by lots of liver and digestion problems.

HARRIS Glenn Milstead (1945–1988), the cross-dressing heavyweight star of many John Waters films known as Divine, may have been plump (estimates weigh in at 370 pounds) but he was always punctual. On the night of March 7, fresh from the critical success of the film *Hairspray* and about to begin work in dual roles on the hit sitcom *Married . . . with Children*, Divine dined with friends. When he returned to his suite at Los Angeles's Regency Hotel, he stepped onto the balcony of Room 261 and sang snatches of "Arrivederci Roma." But when Divine didn't show up on the set, his manager went to the hotel and found his client dead in bed. An autopsy stated that Divine died in his sleep of heart failure, more specifically, an enlarged heart brought on by sleep apnea. He was forty-two years old. His autopsy reports "a large amount of partially digested pasta and other food material" was found in his body.

His family made a simple request: Donate no money to charity in Divine's name, but send flowers, the more the better. Huge arrangements arrived from Elton John and *Polyester* costar Tab Hunter. Whoopi Goldberg's floral tribute included a note that read, "See what a good review will do?" The funniest tribute came from the cast and crew of *Married . . . with Children*. It read: "If you didn't want the job, all you had to do was say so." Divine is buried (under his birth and stage name) in Prospect Hill Park Cemetery in Towson, Maryland.

|||||||||||||||||||||||||||||||||||||||||||||||||||||||||||||||||||||||||||||||||||||||||||||||||||||||||

Popcorn tycoon Orville Redenbacher (1907–1995) didn't go out with a pop but a splash. On September 20, he was found dead in his Jacuzzi at his home in Coronado, California, drowned in the bubbles after suffering a heart attack. He was eighty-eight years old. His body was popped into an oven, cremated, and the ashes scattered at sea. ☻

|||||||||||||||||||||||||||||||||||||||||||||||||||||||||||||||||||||||||||||||||||||||||||||||||||||||||

JAMES Buchanan Brady (1856–1917), may have made headlines with his business savvy (he was the first person to own a car in NYC) and priceless jewel collection, but Diamond Jim really hogged the news with his awesome appetite. A breakfast usually consisted of hominy, eggs, corn bread, muffins, pancakes, pork and/or lamb chops, fried potatoes, beefsteak, and a full gallon of orange juice—a beverage the teetotaler called his "golden nectar." A prelunch snack? Two or three dozen clams and oysters. More clams and oysters were sucked down at lunch, along with boiled lobsters, deviled crabs, a joint of beef, and several kinds of pie. Afternoon tea? A platter of seafood washed down with lemon soda.

But Brady saved his appetite for his major meal of the day: a fifteen-course dinner that included dozens of Maryland oysters, crabs, bowls of green turtle soup, six or seven lobsters, duck, turtle meat, sirloin steak, vegetables, and an entire platter of pastries. And, of course, gallons of OJ. Sometime he'd treat himself to a post-dessert dessert; two pounds of chocolate. He was such a glutton that when once asked what he thought of a certain dish, he quipped, "If you pour sauce over a Turkish towel, I believe I could eat all of it."

The gastrophile died in his sleep of a stroke; an autopsy revealed that his gargantuan stomach was six times larger than that of an average person.

American Psychos

EDWARD Theodore Gein (1906–1984) has made the history books as one scary man. That's because Gein had a most unusual hobby: He'd exhume corpses from local graveyards and make trophies and keepsakes from their bones and skin. His life and crimes have influenced many big-screen madmen, including Norman Bates (*Psycho*) and Buffalo Bill (*The Silence of the Lambs*).

Police caught up with Gein after they suspected him in the disappearance of a hardware store owner. When they entered a shed, there was the store owner's body . . .

decapitated and hung upside down, her wrists and ankles a mass of knotted ropes. Her ribcage had been split and her guts spilled, similar to a dressed deer. A tour of Gein's farmhouse revealed more grim souvenirs, including human skulls mounted as bed corner posts, lampshades and chair seats made of human skin, soup bowls made of skulls, a belt made from several women's nipples, socks made from human flesh, a window shade made of human lips, and a human heart simmering on the stove.

Gein was found guilty of first-degree murder and sentenced to spend the rest of his life in a mental hospital. He died on July 26 of respiratory and heart failure. He is buried in a grave made of stone (not skin or bone) in Plainfield Cemetery in Plainfield, Wisconsin.

CHILDREN fell hook, line, and sinker for the wooing of Albert Fish (1870–1936), who'd bribe the wee ones into the woods, then kill them and cook them in a stew. In 1934, Fish killed and ate ten-year-old Grace Budd, who he had lured into his cottage by inviting her to his niece's fictitious birthday party. He strangled Grace, dismembered her body, and cooked her flesh with onions, peas, and carrots. Her abduction led to a manhunt that lasted for six years, but the police finally netted their Fish from clues contained in an anonymous letter sent to Grace's mom and dad. When Fish was finally caught, he boasted that he had molested and/or eaten "children in every state."

Fish was a sadomasochist and also enjoyed being tortured. One favorite pastime was being whipped and paddled, often with a paddle studded with inch-and-a-half nails. He loved heavy metal, inserting numerous needles into his body, and branded himself with hot irons and pokers. He worked his magic by answering classified ads from lonely hearted women and begging them to torture him; at the time of Fish's death, forty-six of the ad responses were entered as evidence at his trial, but they were so obscene that the prosecution refused to make them public. When the judge sentenced Fish to the electric chair on January 16, 1936, he thanked him. "What a thrill it would be to die! It will be the only thrill I have not tried, the supreme thrill of my life! Thank you, your honor." It took two jolts of juice to kill Fish—the electric chair's current was short-circuited by the myriad needles Fish had inserted into his body.

SO hungry you can eat a horse? How about a fellow human being? Alferd Packer (1842–1907) has gone down in history as "the Colorado Cannibal" for taking a friend to lunch. On April 6, 1874, Parker arrived at the Los Pinos Indian Agency near Gunnison, Colorado—alone. Where were the other five men in his expedition party? Packer wrote a confession, stating that another man, Shannon Bell, killed the others, and that Packer killed Bell in self-defense. And since there was no food—the party had only brought ten days' worth of food—Packer packed it in by eating the dead men's flesh. (Later, when the decaying bodies were found, the area became known as Dead Man's Gulch.)

Packer, who noted that "the breasts of man are the sweetest meat I ever tasted," escaped from jail and went into hiding, living under the alias "John Schwartze" until March 1883, when he was found in Cheyenne, Wyoming. Arrested and returned to Colorado, Packer was tried and sentenced to death. In 1885, his death sentence was reversed by the Colorado Supreme Court and commuted to forty years in prison. In January 1901, then Colorado governor Thomas granted Packer conditional parole. Packer spent the last years of his life as a vegetarian, dying on

April 24, 1907, from a stroke. Since he was a military veteran, he was buried at government expense. The government also paid for his misspelled tombstone that reads, "Alfred Packer, Co. F. 16 U.S. Inf." in Littleton Cemetery in Littleton, Colorado. Packer's legacy continues to provide a feast of popular culture. In 1968, students at the University of Colorado at Boulder named their new cafeteria grill the Alferd G. Packer Memorial Grill with the slogan "Have a friend for lunch!"

The Ultimate Doggie Bag

THE title of one her films sums it up best: Marie Prevost (1898–1937) was *The Beautiful and the Damned*—with an emphasis on "damned." During her twenty-year career, the Canadian-born actress made 121 films, and was one of Mack Sennett's famous Bathing Beauties. But her divorce, alcoholism, and eating problems sent her to the depression doghouse. The end of a brief love affair she had with Howard Hughes made matters worse. And so she drank. And ate. Then drank and ate some more. Her weight gain was so significant that work became scarce. As the fame declined, so did the income. By 1934, there was no work and no money at all.

So Prevost simply stopped eating. She died on January 21, at the age of thirty-eight, from acute alcoholism and extreme malnutrition. Her body was not discovered until two days later, after neighbors complained about her dachshund's incessant barking. A bellboy, ignoring the note Prevost posted on the door asking that no one knock more than once, forced the door open. There was the former beauty, lying facedown on her bed, her legs and arms riddled with tiny bite marks from Maxie in attempts to wake up his mistress. A sea of empty liquor bottles and checks returned for insufficient funds kept them company. So broke was Prevost (her estate was a mere $300) that Joan Crawford paid for her funeral, which was attended by a bevy of stars, including Crawford, Clark Gable, Wallace Beery, and Barbara Stanwyck.

Her death did some good—the founding of the Motion Picture and Television Country House and Hospital, which continues to provide medical care for employees of the television and motion picture industry. Her death was also creative fodder. British musician Nick Lowe's satirical song "Marie Provost" (the misspelling is his) includes the refrain "She was a winner / Who became the doggie's dinner."

Animal Planet

CREATURE DISCOMFORTS

Are You *Sure* This Is Crunchy Peanut Butter?

JUMBO (1861–1885) the thirteen-foot tall elephant had quite the circus career thanks to all of P. T. Barnum's ballyhooing. But even the big and mighty meet the Grim Reaper—and sometimes not in the most glamorous of ways. In 1885, Jumbo was crushed by a locomotive at a Canadian train yard. A necropsy was done, and many metallic objects were found in Jumbo's stomach, including pennies, nickels, dimes, keys, and rivets. His skeleton was donated to the American Museum of Natural History in New York City; his heart was sold to Cornell University. Jumbo's hide was stuffed and the mounted specimen traveled with Barnum's circus for many years. In 1889, Barnum donated the stuffed Jumbo to Boston's Tufts University, where it was displayed until destroyed by a 1975 fire. The remaining ashes are kept in a fourteen-ounce Peter Pan crunchy peanut butter jar in the office of the Tufts athletic director (since 1975, teammates have rubbed the jar for good luck); his taxidermied tail also resides at Tufts, in an acid-free cardboard box.

Hog Heaven

TV fans went hog wild over Arnold Ziffel (1964–1972), the female pig that starred opposite Eva Gabor and Eddie Albert on *Green Acres*. Several females portrayed Arnold; each was replaced as she grew too big for the part. This was one smart pig: Arnold could play piano, write her name, change channels on the TV, play cricket with a bat, even drink from a straw. Gabor hated the swine star—"He's a dirty beast!" she often exclaimed. Maybe she was pissed Arnold got more fan mail than she did?

Arnold was trained by Frank Inn (1916–2002), who worked his magic with numerous four-footed celebs. His illustrious career began by accident . . . a very eerie accident. When Inn was nineteen, he was hit by a car and pronounced dead. A student at the morgue was about to prepare the autopsy when he realized that Inn's heart was beating. An ambulance whizzed him to the hospital where, while recuperating, he adopted a puppy he named Jeep, which he taught a few tricks, launching him on a sixty-year career as a trainer.

When the original Arnold died, she was cremated and the ashes placed in an urn that Inn kept. When Inn died, Arnold's ashes were placed in his casket. Also lining Inn's casket: the ashes of canine stars Benji (1957–1975) and Tramp, the latter of whom starred on *My Three Sons*. All the beasts rest quite contently at Forest Lawn Memorial Park in Hollywood Hills, California.

Whale of a Tale

KEIKO the orca whale (1977–2003) swam to stardom as the lead in *Free Willy* and its two sequels. He was free, free at last, after dying of acute pneumonia on December 12 in the Taknes fjord of Norway at the age of twenty-seven.

Keiko's rise to stardom is the stuff of which hit films are made. Born in the Atlantic Ocean near Iceland, he was captured by a fishing boat and separated from his family. In 1982, a Canadian marine park bought him and trained him to perform. Three years later, the whale—now named Keiko, which means "Lucky One" in Japanese—was sold to an amusement park in Mexico City for $350,000. In 1992, Warner Brothers spent $20 million making the film in which a young boy befriends a captive killer whale. Keiko even made the cover of *Life*.

But Willy was sick, and the outcry from the public over his deplorable living conditions helped generate millions of dollars in hopes of returning him to the wild. On January 7, 1996, the 7,720-pound whale was airlifted by United Parcel Service to a rehabilitation facility at the Oregon Coast Aquarium that cost $7.3 million to build.

On September 9, 1998, the orca was flown to Iceland in preparation for his eventual release, but five years later, Keiko/Willy, now weighing in at 9,620 pounds, showed signs of lethargy. He wasn't eating and his respiratory rate was irregular. With little warning, he beached himself and died in the early evening. The pet's vets believe that Keiko, buried at Taknes Bay in Taknes Bay, Norway, was the second oldest male orca ever in captivity.

Old Rip, RIP

SOME toads have all the luck. Back in 1897, a horned toad was placed in the cornerstone of the courthouse in Eastland, Texas, as it was being sealed. On February 18, 1928, as the courthouse was being demolished, the dusty toad resurfaced . . . still alive!

Nicknamed "Old Rip," he found a press agent and went on tour, even getting to sit on the desk of President Calvin Coolidge. Less than a year after the miraculous discovery, the toad finally croaked of pneumonia. His body is on display in a tiny, velvet-lined open casket in the lobby of the new courthouse.

Life with a Porpoise

IN yet another one of Hollywood's sex switches, the splashy male star known as Flipper was actually a gal known as Mitzi (1958–1972). She/he played the title role in the 1963 film *Flipper*, then went on to star in the TV series for four years. She died of a heart attack at the age of fourteen. Mitzi is interred in the courtyard of the school at the Dolphin Research Institute and Center on Grassy Key, in the Florida Keys about two miles south of Miami. Her grave marked by a statue of a life-size dolphin.

Ruff-ing It Out

BEING in the doghouse was never so lovely. Canine star Rin Tin Tin (1918–1932), the screen's first four-legged superstar, was fourteen when he was discovered by American servicemen in a bombed-out dog kennel in Lorraine, France, less than two months before the end of World War I. Rin Tin Tin's films were so successful they saved Warner Brothers from bankruptcy. After a successful screen career, the German shepherd's luck ran out on August 10. He died in the arms of Jean Harlow, who lived across the street from the dog's trainer, Lee Duncan. Upon his death, the dog was buried in the backyard of the Duncan home; later his body was returned to the country of his birth, and he is buried in Lile aux Chiens in Asnieres, France.

Shocking News

CALL this one a case of topsy-turvy. Topsy (1875–1903), a featured pachyderm player with a circus at Coney Island's Luna Park, may not have been as domesticated as people first believed. After killing three men in as many years, Topsy was branded Trouble . . . and given the death sentence. She was sentenced to hang, but the Society for the Prevention of Cruelty to Animals objected, saying such treatment would be inhumane. So Thomas Alva Edison stepped in, suggesting electrocuting Topsy. At the time, he was engaged in battle with George Westinghouse for control of America's electric infrastructure. Good ol' Thomas Alva declared that his direct current system was safe, but that Westinghouse's alternating current was deadly. How deadly? To prove his theory, Edison had been publicly electrocuting dogs and cats for years.

And now it was Topsy's turn. He was led to a special-built platform; just in case the deadly 6,600-volt charge didn't do the job, Topsy was fed carrots laced with 400 grams of potassium cyanide. Wooden sandals with copper electrodes were attached to her feet.

The signal was given, and at 2:45 p.m. on January 4, Edison's men threw the switch. There was a bit of smoke, Topsy raised her trunk, bent her knee, and all six tons of her fell onto her right side. She was dead, a cruel ten-second act caught on film by Edison, and an event witnessed by fifteen hundred people. She was dissected on the spot, with her hide being sold for commercial purposes and her feet sold to make umbrella stands.

Topsy's obituary made page 1 of the *New York Times*, and Edison would later release the footage under the title "Electrocuting an Elephant." We hear 'phant fans are still giving it two trunks down.

Gone Ape

RONALD Reagan's most famous costar was shorter, funnier, and a lot hairier than Nancy. Her name was Peggy (?–1951), but film fans know her as Bonzo, the chimpanzee who starred opposite Reagan in the 1951 camp classic, *Bedtime for Bonzo.*

Bonzo's real bedtime came that same year when a fire swept through a Quonset hut in which she and her three stand-in chimps were resting. They were waiting to appear with the future president on what was the first PATSY Award ceremony—the animal equivalent to the Oscar. Bonzo survived the flames (not one singed strand of fur) but died from smoke inhalation, despite a thirty-minute resuscitation attempt. She is spending eternity monkeying around at Hearthside Rest Pet Cemetery in McKean, Pennsylvania, in a grave (erroneously) marked "He Made Us Laugh."

Hides, Now Go Seek

LET'S get the most important stuff out of the way first: Trigger (1932–1965), Roy Roger's trusty golden palomino that he rode in every one of his 188 films, was not stuffed. He was mounted. The horse's hide was stretched, quite tightly, over a plaster likeness and left to dry. Today, Trigger—reared on his hind legs with a silver saddle on his back and a bit and bridle in place—greets the hundreds of thousands of visitors who visit the Roy Rogers/Dale Evans Museum in Branson, Missouri. Trigger is not the only Rogers relic on display: There's also Buttermilk (Dale Evans's pearl-colored quarter horse), Bullet (the Rogerses' German shepherd), and Trigger Jr. And no, Roy (1911–1998) and Dale (1912–2001) are not mounted or buried here. They are on display at Sunset Hills Memorial Park in Apple Valley, California.

So if Trigger's hide was used, whatever happened to the

rest of him? His meat had been illegally sold to several small eateries in the southwest and butcher John L. Jones was sentenced to five years in prison.

". . . and Your Little Dog, Too!"

THE world's most recognizable cairn terrier was a girl named Terry (1933–1943), yet her most famous role was playing a boy, Toto, in *The Wizard of Oz*. Terry, who had been abandoned as a pup, was trained by canine coach Carl Spitz, who put the pooch through her paces with a series of innovative hand signals. When she wasn't working (and she worked often, popping up in credited roles in thirteen other movies), Terry lived at Spitz's kennel just outside Los Angeles. She earned $125 a week for her work as Judy Garland's big-screen furry friend, a good deal more than the $50 per week the Singer Midgets were paid for their roles as the Munchkins. (Toto, who is in more scenes than Judy, barks forty-four times in the film.)

When Terry died at ten, she was buried in a special area behind the Spitz's kennel. Don't expect to find it, even if you have magical red ruby slippers. During the expansion of the Ventura Freeway, Spitz's property was bought for construction purposes, and the Spitz kennel, school, and burial grounds were destroyed. There's no place like home, unless it's ruled by eminent domain.

Till Death Do Them Part

FATAL FAMILY ATTRACTIONS

Marital Blitz

PROFESSIONAL wrestler Chris Benoit (1967–2007) certainly wrestled with inner demons. On June 25, 2007, he called the office of World Wrestling Entertainment to say he would be "late" for a fight that evening. Worried since Benoit had missed other appointments and had sent "several curious text messages," WWE officials asked the Sheriff's Department to check on Benoit. They found more blood than ever found in any wrestling ring: The five-foot, eleven-inch, 220-pound Benoit had spent three days committing heinous crimes—murdering his wife Nancy on Friday, strangling his son Daniel on Saturday, then wrapping a cord from an exercise machine around his neck and hanging himself in the basement on Sunday. By the time Nancy was found—in an upstairs bedroom, with her wrists and feet bound and her body wrapped in a towel—rigor mortis had set in, and her skin was "marbleized" as she lay facedown on the floor. Posters of his dad were hanging in

Daniel's room, and two toy wrestling belts sat on a shelf. A Bible was left next to each body. Toxicology reports indicated that the former WWE champion had steroids, testosterone, and other drugs in his body at the time of the murders/suicide. The reports also stated that mother and son had been sedated with Xanax before they were killed; Daniel also had needle marks on his arms, which have never been explained.

Benoit's father, Michael Benoit, allowed a neurosurgery expert to dissect his son's brain; results showed that the years of wrestling caused repeated, untreated concussions and that Benoit's brain was so severely damaged in all four lobes and the brain stem that it resembled the brain of an eighty-five-year-old Alzheimer's patient. His brain also showed an advanced form of dementia, caused by dead brain cells as a result of head trauma.

THE names of Chaplin and Keaton and Lloyd and Arbuckle are more familiar, but film history credits silent-screen clown Max Linder (1883–1925) with the invention of slapstick comedy. The French-born clown made some five hundred films, and sadly only bits and pieces of about eighty-two survive. Even sadder is that Linder is remembered for the sensational way he and his actress/model wife, Helene Peters died—in a murder/suicide pact. Their first attempt failed in early 1924 (it was covered up by a physician who reported it as an accidental overdose of "sleeping powder"); however, on October 31, the couple was successful, After taking morphine, Max slashed Helene's wrists, then his own. Two suicide notes were found at the scene, their contents never revealed. The headlines were sensational, with a front-page *New York Times* obit gushing, "Max Linder and Wife in Double Suicide; They Drink Veronal, Inject Morphine and Open Veins in Their Arms." Gee, and we thought the *National Enquirer* was tacky.

* * *

SELF-CONFESSED class clown Philip Edward Hartman (1948–1998) knew how funny life could be. The former Groundlings member spent eight years as a cast member on *Saturday Night Live* and provided the voices for Lionel Hutz and Troy McClure in the animated sitcom *The Simpsons*. So what went wrong, shortly before 3 a.m. on May 28 when police were summoned to his Encino, California, home after a 911 report of shots being fired? The actor's intoxicated and drugged wife, Brynn Hartman (1958–1998), had loaded three slugs into her hubby as he slept in boxer shorts and a white T-shirt. She then managed to drive to a friend's house and confessed to the crime. She and the friend drove back to the murder site; when he called 911, she barricaded herself (along with her dead husband) in the master bedroom then shot herself once in the head. Toxicology reports showed that Brynn had a blood alcohol level of approximately .12 percent; there were also significant amounts of cocaine and antidepressants in her system. The reason for such a mess? The story was that Phil was planning to tell Brynn he was leaving her because of her drug addiction, but no one knows for sure; the truth was sprinkled over Catalina Island's Emerald Bay, along with their ashes.

WE know that sex can bring out the beast in some men, but in the case of Paul Snider (1951–1980) it brought more. Much more. October 1979 *Playboy* model and actress Dorothy Stratten (1960–1980) had decided to tell her husband Snider, whom she met while she was working at a Canadian Dairy Queen, that she was severing their relationship. Snider was a control freak, forbidding his wife to drink coffee because it would stain her teeth, and even poisoning her dog because he was jealous of their relationship. On August 14, Dorothy had flown in from New York and met

Paul at his apartment. She had $1,000 in her handbag that she was going to give to Snider to go away.

Snider cashed in all right. A day passed, then another, with no word from the apartment. A neighbor entered and found a scene straight out of a horror film. Stratten's nude body was lying facedown, covered in blood. Two bloody handprints were on her buttocks. One finger of her left hand was missing. So was much of her face. Snider was lying next to her, his naked body boasting a gaping hole where his eyes had been. There was a third victim, of sorts. The coroner would later deem it a "love contraption" for "possible rear entry intercourse"—designed by Snider, it was a bondage bench that he was hoping to sell to the porn industry . . . and the bench onto which he had strapped Stratten with medical tape, having intercourse with her bloody corpse for a half hour before shooting himself.

Stratten was dead at the age of twenty and was buried in Westwood Memorial Park in Los Angeles. Director Peter Bogdanovich, with whom she was romantically involved at the time, wrote the quixotic epitaph that appears on her gravestone ("If people bring so much courage to this world the world has to kill them to break them . . ."). Snider's body was exported to his native Canada, where he's interred in Schara Tzedeck Cemetery in Vancouver.

HE starred in many films and TV shows, but October 19 was the final gig for Gig Young (1913–1978). Just three weeks after his fifth marriage to twenty-one-year-old German actress Kim Schmidt—they met on the set of the 1978 Bruce Lee film *Game of Death*—the couple starred in a real game of death: a murder/suicide. When police found them in Apartment 1BB of New York City's ritzy Osborne Apartments, she had a bullet hole from a .38-caliber

Smith & Wesson in her skull; he had shot her, then stuck the gun barrel in his own mouth. The Youngs were found about five hours after the crime, when the groceries Kim had ordered were noticed still sitting in the lobby. Gig's blood-soaked diary was open to September 27, 1978, the day of their marriage. Hey, at least he remembered the date.

Survey Says

FAME! Fortune! Money! His own TV show! All good answers to Ray Combs (1956–1996), the host of *Family Feud* from 1988 to 1993. A year after the show went off the air, however, things began to change. Combs was severely injured in a car accident that nearly paralyzed him and caused him constant back problems. His attempts to return to the small screen were short-lived; he opened a comedy club that quickly closed. Then came the financial problems; the man who had earned more than $6 million a year was now in debt, and the bank foreclosed on one of his homes.

A deeply depressed Combs was admitted to the psych ward of California's Glendale Medical Center. It was determined that he was suicidal and a danger to others, so he was placed on a seventy-two-hour suicide watch. But no one was watching. At 4:07 on the morning of June 2, Combs removed the sheets from his bed and hanged himself in a closet.

The forty-year-old was laid to rest in Greenwood Cemetery in Hamilton, Ohio, where fans can easily spot his grave by the engraved image of Combs smiling at them. The $25,000 funeral and gravestone were paid for by—survey says—Johnny Carson, one of Combs's idols.

A Rose Is a Rose Is a Rose . . . Until It Dies

THE curtain rose one last time on the life of British actor George Rose (1920–1988) on a chilly, gray June morning in 1988 when nearly eight hundred people gathered at New York City's Shubert Theater to pay homage to the actor Jack Lemmon claimed had given him the most pleasure in theater, the actor of whom Katharine Hepburn said, "It may be my name that brings them in, but it's George Rose that gets them going."

In 1984, Rose purchased a large three-bedroom home on the north coast of the Dominican Republic. The openly gay actor so wanted a family that he took in a fourteen-year-old Dominican boy named Domingo (Juan) Vásquez. He supported him financially and was rumored to have a sexual relationship with him. He adopted the boy in 1986, naming Juan heir to his $2 million estate.

In 1988, Rose's body was found beside his overturned car in a ditch, off the main road near his home. He had been beaten to death by his adopted son and three other men, including Vasquez's father and uncle, who tried to make the death look like the result of a car crash. The assailants confessed to taking Rose to a field and torturing him for eight hours before killing him. The four men were charged with murder and spent some time in prison, but since an actual trial was never held, they were eventually released. Rose is buried in an unmarked grave in a cemetery that could easily pass for a junkyard.

Oedipus Wrecks

SCREEN siren Susan Cabot (1926–1986) made her film debut in the 1947 noir gem *Kiss of Death*. Her death, nearly forty years later, could, in a most warped way, be construed as a final kiss of death. The five-foot, two-inch tall actress was bludgeoned to death by her dwarf son, Timothy Scott Roman. (His father was said to be King Hussein of Jordan, with whom Susan had a well-publicized affair in 1959. He cut off their relationship when he found out that Cabot was Jewish.)

At 10:30 on the evening of December 10, Timothy called police to report an intruder had broken into their Encino, California, home. He told them that "a tall Latino with curly hair, dressed like a Japanese Ninja warrior" attacked him and Cabot and made off with $70,000 cash. The tiny terror also said he fought with Mr. Ninja but was knocked out. Good story save a few things: Timothy had a mere bruise on his head and a teeny cut on his arm. Four Akitas were guarding Cabot's bedroom, and Timothy wasn't allowing the police behind closed doors.

When the bedroom door was finally broken down, Cabot was found lying in bed on her stomach, her body clad in a purple nightgown. A blood-soaked sheet covered her head, and blood, brain, and skull matter were spattered on the mirrored walls and ceiling. Timothy was charged with the murder; his lawyers claimed that the experimental growth hormone Timothy had been taking for fifteen years left him a bit "unstable."

The murder weapon? A dumbbell that the dwarf hid in a box of Bold 3 laundry detergent. Timothy got a three-year suspended sentence (no one could prove that the murder was premeditated). She got an unmarked grave at Hillside Memorial Park in Culver City.

Knocking 'Em Dead

THE SHOW REALLY GOES ON

Final Regards to Broadway

GOWER Champion (1919–1980), the director of the Carol Channing blockbuster *Hello, Dolly!*, was a trouper to the end. The very end. Though he was gravely ill (and knew it), Tony-winning Champion championed on, relentlessly working as director and choreographer on the 1980 musical *42nd Street*. A few days before the show opened on Broadway, Champion was admitted to Manhattan's Memorial Sloan-Kettering Cancer Center and diagnosed with a rare and terminal cancer of the blood known as Waldenstrom's macroglobulinemia. The play opened as scheduled; immediately after the ten curtain calls that August 25, producer David Merrick walked out from the wings to make the stunning announcement "Our beloved director Gower Champion has died." Champion had died hours before the curtain went up, but Merrick managed to keep the tragedy a secret. Champion's life ran fifty-nine years. *42nd Street* ran 3,486 performances.

Channing remembers David Burns (1902–1971), her

Hello, Dolly! costar (he played the original Horace Van-dergelder), as "a round-faced, wise-cracking genius." Those who were performing with Burns during "Go Visit Your Grandmother," a musical number he was performing during a Philadelphia tryout of the Broadway-bound *70, Girls, 70*, remember him as alive . . . then dead. At 10 p.m., during a performance, Burns collapsed onstage, dying soon afterwards of a heart attack. "He had just gotten a laugh," Channing recalls. "And when he didn't get up, the audience laughed even louder. Imagine! Getting such a favorable reaction on your final exit."

TINY Tim (1932–1996) listened to no one. In September 1996, he suffered a heart attack just as he began performing at a ukulele festival in Massachusetts. He was hospitalized for three weeks and warned that he should retire from performing since he was suffering from acute heart and diabetic problems. On November 30, he was playing his trademark "Tiptoe through the Tulips" at a women's club benefit in Minneapolis. He suffered another heart attack; when his third wife asked him if he was okay, he said, "No, I'm not!" He collapsed and was rushed to the hospital, where doctors tried to resuscitate him for seventy-five minutes. He is buried with his ukulele.

HIS season of love lasted thirty-five years, until an aortic aneurysm suddenly snatched away the life of playwright/composer Jonathan Larson (1960–1996), who died the night before off-Broadway previews of his musical *Rent* began.

Larson lived in an unheated fifth-floor Lower Manhattan loft and dreamt of the day he could afford cable TV. He spent seven years working on the show, waiting tables to support himself and quitting the job just two months before

Rent opened. He was so broke that just ten days before he died he sold some of his books at a New York bookstore to buy a movie ticket.

On Sunday, January 21, after eating dinner and reportedly smoking pot, Larson nearly collapsed backstage. Dizzy and short of breath, he told a friend his chest was "killing" him. An ambulance rushed him to Cabrini Medical Center's emergency room. At 7 p.m., Larson underwent an electrocardiogram; two doctors blamed the pain on stress. Before leaving the hospital, after telling doctors "I can't take a breath," Larson had his stomach pumped and was given fifty grains of charcoal "to absorb toxins." He was urged to follow a bland diet for twenty-four hours. A few days later, more pain. Another trip to a different hospital. Doctors insisted he had the flu since X-rays and EKGS showed nothing abnormal.

While *Rent* was in rehearsals, a pale Larson popped in the theater now and then. Four days later, on January 25, at about 3:30 a.m., one of his roommates found Larson lying on the kitchen floor. Medics declared him dead on the spot. The autopsy report states that the official cause of death was from "aortic dissection due to cystic medial degeneration of unknown etiology"—a rip in his main blood vessel. Larson was buried in Snyder Cemetery in Albany, New York, and his work (and death) did not go unrecognized: He was awarded a posthumous Pulitzer and four Tony Awards for *Rent*.

IT was April 17, and he was having fun and getting lots of laughs. Comedian Dick Shawn (1923–1987) was cutting up a San Diego crowd, reciting campaign clichés such as "If elected, I will not lay down on the job." So when he fell facedown on the stage, the audience thought it was part of the act and they hooted and hollered some more. Then too much time passed, Shawn refused to get up, and the crowd started to boo. The next day they would learn that the comic had suffered a massive heart attack and had died.

A Final Word from Their Sponsor

LUCILLE Ball found him hilarious. His *Three's Company* co-star Suzanne Somers called him a "genius." The paramedics had a different word for John Ritter (1948–2003): deceased. During rehearsals for an episode of his TV sitcom *8 Simple Rules for Dating My Teenage Daughter*, the comedian began feeling ill then suddenly collapsed. Guest star Henry Winkler remembers that Ritter seemed fine in the morning, but by afternoon, his friend was "sweating badly. He told me, 'I really need to get some water.' That was the last time I saw him." Ritter was rushed to Providence Saint Joseph Medical Center, where at 10:40 p.m., he was pronounced dead of an "aortic dissection," a tear in the aorta that can occur without warning. ABC renamed the show *8 Simple Rules*; Ritter's character died after collapsing in a grocery store. But Ritter's death left a void, and the show was cancelled in early 2005. (Ritter received a posthumous Emmy nomination; he lost to *Frasier* star Kelsey Grammer who paid tribute to Ritter in his acceptance speech.)

Then, there was the aftermath—played out in court. Ritter's widow, Amy Yasbeck, filed a $67 million wrongful death suit against doctors Matthew Lotysch and Joseph Lee, alleging that they misdiagnosed her hubby's condition. (She chose that number, she says, because "that's what John would have made over the rest of his lifetime.") In March 2008, a month after the trial started in Los Angeles County Superior Court, the doctors were found not responsible for Ritter's death by a jury vote of 9–3. Widow Ritter did receive $9.4 million from Providence Saint Joseph Medical Center. Hopefully, Ritter is finally at peace, in his grave at Forest Lawn in Hollywood Hills. Once asked how he wanted to be remembered, he said, "Just as a guy who was interested in the golden thread that intertwines all of us together. You know, that golden thread that goes through me and you. It either makes you laugh or it makes you cry—I'd like to be remembered as a guy who plucked a few of those golden threads of humanity."

IT'S not easy being green. But there's something to be said about being prepared when you're in the pink. Four years before his death, while on vacation, Jim Henson (1936–1990) wrote letters to his five children, asking that they only be opened upon his death. Inside were instructions for his funeral, which were followed when the fifty-three-year-old Henson died on May 16, at 12:58 a.m. His organs had shut down as the result of a severe bacterial infection.

Two separate memorial services were held for the Muppet Master, one in New York City and one in London, England. Henson requested "a nice, friendly little service," with no one wearing black and a "rousing" Dixieland jazz band performing "When the Saints Go Marching In." Funeral programs were printed with Henson's own declaration: "Please watch out for each other and love and forgive everybody. It's a good life, enjoy it."

As Harry Belafonte sang, each member of the audience waved a puppeteer's rod attached to brightly colored foam butterflies. Son Brian read portions of the letters his dad had written those years earlier: "Don't feel bad that I've gone. I look forward to seeing all of you when you come over."

REDD Foxx (1922–1991) was tickled pink. Yes, he owed the IRS money (they had raided his Las Vegas home and seized almost all his assets for back taxes, penalties, and interest in excess of three million dollars) but he was back on TV with the sitcom *The Royal Family*, doing what he loved:

comedy. His costar was his good chum Della Reese. On October 11, during a break from rehearsals, the raspy-voiced Foxx, who had complained of chills earlier, fell to the floor. Della and crew thought he was spoofing his famous *Sanford and Son* heart attack bit . . . but this time the funny man wasn't being funny. Della began to pray, begging her friend not to die. Foxx was rushed to Hollywood Presbyterian Hospital, where he was pronounced dead at 7:45 p.m.

IRENE Ryan (1902–1973) died at the age of seventy, several days following a stroke suffered during a performance of the Broadway musical *Pippin*. (She knew she had a brain tumor, but the show does go on.) Pallbearers at her funeral included *Beverly Hillbillies* costars Buddy Ebsen and Max Baer Jr. Ryan's tombstone at Woodlawn Cemetery in Santa Monica, California, reminds visitors she played "Granny."

CARMEN Miranda (1909–1955), the gal in the tutti-frutti hat, suffered a heart attack during a segment of the live *Jimmy Durante Show* on August 4. She completed her dance number and nearly collapsed. At the end of the show, she smiled, waved to her fans, and left for home, dying later that night of a second heart attack.

Suicide Ain't Painless . . .

BUT IT SURE IS MESSY

Oops!

SOME people are *waaaay* out there. Marshall Applewhite (1931–1997) was certain that a spaceship was trailing the Hale-Bopp Comet, so he convinced his thirty-eight followers to commit suicide so that their souls could board. In a videotape later made public, the kooky Heaven's Gate cult leader said that he believed mass suicide "was the only way to evacuate this Earth." So off they went, tummies filled with phenobarbital, cyanide, and arsenic that had been mixed with applesauce and pudding, and then washed down with vodka, clutching to the belief that a UFO would take their souls to another "level of existence above human." The members also placed plastic bags over their heads just in case the drugs didn't do the trick. The massive death scene took place over three days. Police found the bodies, each wearing black Nike sneakers, rotting in the heat of the Rancho Santa Fe, California, sun. It took balls to play follow the leader, even if six males had been castrated as well. Taste a bit of irony: One of the victims was the younger brother of *Star Trek* actress Nichelle Nichols. What to do with such a mess? President Clinton ordered them all cremated.

IT'S a lesson matinee idol Lou Tellegen (1883–1934) should have learned. The actor began his career on the stage in his native Holland, becoming the toast of Paris by 1909. He and famed actress Sarah Bernhardt began a torrid affair, even though she was thirty-seven years his senior. Hollywood beckoned, and the handsome actor made nearly four dozen films. Then talkies and cancer entered the frame. Gravely ill, bankrupt, out of work, his handsome face scarred by a fire, he decided to go out in style. In the bathroom of the mansion in which he was a guest, he stood in the front of the mirror, shaved, powdered his face, then took a pair of gold scissors—on which his name was engraved—and stabbed himself in the heart seven times. He had fallen into such obscurity that when reporters telephoned his former wife, opera diva Geraldine Farrar, asking for a comment on Tellegen's death, she said, "Why should that interest me?" Only thirty-seven family and friends showed up for the funeral of an actor whose fan base once boasted millions.

Too Quick on the Trigger

IT'S something even Oprah hasn't tried. Christine Chubbuck (1944–1974) was a well-liked TV reporter who happened to suffer from depression. On July 15, about eight minutes into reporting local news on the morning show, she switched gears. Looking into the camera, she slowly said, "In keeping with Channel 40's policy of bringing you the latest in blood and guts, and in living color, you are going to see another first: an attempted suicide." She then lifted a .38, hidden in a bag under her desk, and pointed it at the lower part of her head and fired. Her hair flew about as the smoke rose. Her head shook and her body slumped against her desk then onto the floor. TV crews quickly slapped a public service tape, then a movie, into play. Her associates would later find blood-soaked news accounts about the suicide on Chubbock's desk and in her hand. It was also later revealed that Chubbuck had called the local police department, and in the guise of doing story research, asked about the best way to kill oneself with a gun. She was told the .38 needed to be placed at the back of the head and the slug should be a wadcutter, which would disintegrate and cause certain damage. Her ashes were sprinkled over the Gulf of Mexico three days later. No one was there to film it.

SUCH an animated lady! And such a sad one. Mary Kay Bergman (1961-1999) lent her vocal talents to many female characters on the cartoon series *South Park*, as well as supplying the voice of Snow White in modern-day TV cartoons and DVDs. Bergman was last seen alive around 9 p.m. the day of her death. When her husband and a friend returned home, they found Mary Kay, a suicide note, and a Mossberg 12-gauge shotgun. The thirty-eight-year-old actress had shoved the barrel against her forehead just above her nose. The voice of Mrs. Butterworth was stilled at 10:18 p.m. Her grave at Forest Lawn in Hollywood Hills is festooned with some of her *South Park* creations.

WHAT some people won't do for a little attention. Take the case of Pennsylvania politician Robert "Budd" Dwyer (1939–1987), who, on January 22, the day before his sentencing for charges of bribery, conspiracy to commit fraud, and five counts of mail fraud called a press conference—many assumed he was going to resign as state treasurer.

The nervous Dwyer again professed his innocence, and declared that he would not resign. "I thank the good Lord for giving me 47 years of exciting challenges, stimulating experiences, many happy occasions, and, most of all, the finest wife and children any man could ever desire," he said. "I face a maximum sentence of 55 years in prison and a $300,000 fine for being innocent."

He went on, stopping at one point to give three staff members each an envelope. Dwyer then opened a manila envelope and withdrew a .357 Magnum revolver, requesting "Please leave the room if this will offend you." Despite the cries of those wanting to help, Dwyer put the gun barrel into his mouth and pulled the trigger. He collapsed against a wall in a sitting position. Blood poured from his nose and the top of his head. The suicide was caught on film by five TV cameras.

What were in the three envelopes? One contained a suicide note to his wife, one an organ donor card, and one a letter to Pennsylvania governor Robert P. Casey, who had taken office only two days before.

Falling from Grace

ELIZABETH Hartman (1943–1987) is best remembered as Selina D'Arcy, the blind girl who falls for Sidney Poitier in *A Patch of Blue*. Hartman hit it big, fast. She was just twenty-two when she earned an Oscar nomination for the 1965 film that marked her movie debut—at the time, the youngest ever in the category of Best Actress. (She lost to Julie Christie for *Darling*, but did get a Golden Globe.)

But Liz's biggest costar was acute depression. It interfered with her work and she lost parts. Her last role was the voice of a mouse in the 1982 animated flick *The Secret of NIMH*. By now, her fifteen-year marriage had crumbled, and she disappeared from view. But she popped up one last time on Wednesday, June 10, when her body was found on the sidewalk, five floors below the window of the Pittsburgh apartment in which she had been living. At the time Hartman was an outpatient at a psychiatric hospital and called her doctor seeking emergency help the morning of her suicide. He assured her not to worry. Not one celebrity attended her funeral. She rests alongside her mother in a Youngstown, Ohio, patch of green.

SHE died too young for any real critical assessment of her work, but one thing's for sure: Peggy Entwistle (1908–1932) could climb. And climb she did, on September 18, when, after a night of heavy drinking, the Depression-era starlet made for the illuminated HOLLYWOODLAND sign. (The "LAND" section was officially removed in 1949.) Unhappy with the way her career was heading, she decided to go out in a way everyone would remember. Peg climbed up the slope to reach the sign, neatly folded her coat, and placed it with her handbag at the base of a maintenance ladder. She climbed fifty feet up an electrician's ladder to the top of the letter *H*, said farewell to the town that spurned her and took a dive while the sign's five thousand bulbs blinked. Her fall was letter-perfect and she died instantly.

The suicide note found in her handbag read: "I am afraid I am a coward. I am sorry for everything. If I had done this a long time ago, it would have saved a lot of pain. P.E." Since Peg didn't sign the note, police didn't know who the dead woman was. Peg's note was published in several newspapers in the hope that someone would recognize the writing and initials. Indeed, it was her uncle who did travel to Hollywood, where he identified her body in the morgue.

How was she to know that if she'd waited a few more days, she'd receive a letter offering her a starring role in a

Beverly Hills Playhouse production . . . about a woman driven to suicide?

HER face had graced the covers of *Vogue* and *Elle*, and had appeared in ads for Nina Ricci, DKNY, Vera Wang, and Christian Dior, but there she was, now gracing the blacktop of Water Street in the Financial District of New York City. The green-eyed Russian supermodel Ruslana Korshunova (1987–2008), known as "the Russian Rapunzel" for her long, flowing chestnut locks, was dead, yet still fashionable, wearing jeans and a tank top when she decided to end it all with a leap at 2:30 in the afternoon. Just days from her twenty-first birthday, she jumped from the ninth-floor balcony of her apartment building, ripping out the construction netting that was marking an upcoming job. One witness recalls, "her arms were crushed, and her head was on the left side and blood was coming out in a pool." Police called it a suicide though no suicide note was left; friends report that she was distraught over the breakup of a relationship. She was buried on July 7 in Khovanskoye Cemetery in Moscow because, her mother told reporters, the Russian capital was one of her daughter's favorite cities.

AND then there's Maude . . . Anyone who sings along with the theme to the hit TV series starring Bea Arthur (1922–2009) knows the man they are singing with is Donny Hathaway (1945–1979). What they may not know: A year after the show ended its run, Hathaway had dinner with his manager at pal Roberta Flack's New York apartment on January 13, then returned to his room at the Essex House. He removed the glass from a window and leaped fifteen floors to his death.

IN a short career, Leslie Cheung (1956–2003) appeared in more than sixty films, most notably 1993's *Farewell*

My Concubine. Ironically, the gay Chinese actor/singer's last film was *Inner Senses*, a 2002 flop in which his character kills himself. A year later, on the night of April 1, Cheung actually did kill himself by jumping from the balcony of his suite on the twenty-fourth floor of Hong Kong's Mandarin Oriental Hotel. A suicide note addressed to his lover, banker Tong Hock Tak—who later admitted Leslie was seeing a shrink for depression—was found in a pocket. It read, "I have not done one single bad thing in my life. Why is it like that?" No April Fool was he.

FRENCH actress Capucine (1928–1990)—Simone Clouseau in the 1963 comedy *The Pink Panther*—certainly didn't have nine lives. On March 17, the willowy model-turned-actress walked on the wild side and jumped to her death from a window of her eighth-floor apartment in Lausanne, Switzerland. She was survived by her three cats, not a pink panther among them.

CHILDREN not only say the darndest things, they do the darndest as well. Case in point: Diane Linkletter (1948–1969), the daughter of TV personality and author Art Linkletter. On October 4, after making cookies and reading *The Story of O*, the twenty-year-old jumped out of the kitchen window of Apartment 610 at the Shoreham Towers, a fancy high-rise in West Hollywood. Police found $14.66 in cash and some credit cards in the pocket of the jeans she was wearing. She died on arrival at the hospital, at 10:04 a.m. Rumors immediately began to swirl that Linkletter had taken massive amounts of LSD before her spontaneous flight. Great copy—especially after her own papa blamed the hallucinogen for her death, remarking that she took "a much stronger dose of this poison than she should have." Then came the Los Angeles Coroner's report: Linkletter died from "cerebral contusions, extensive, as well as massive skull fracture and multiple fractures of extremities" . . . she had no drugs in her system at the time. (Art responded by stating that she was suffering from an "LSD flashback.")

Diane may have been unknown until she hit the ground, but that soon changed. She and her dad won the 1970 Grammy Award for Best Spoken Word Recording for a ditty entitled "We Love You, Call Collect" on which a worried dad pleads with his runaway daughter. (He: "Come back! Come back!" She: "I gotta do what's right for me." He: "We love you. Call collect.") Recorded the April before her death, it was released by Capitol Records the month after she died, selling a staggering 275,000 copies in eight weeks. The royalties from the sales went "to combat problems arising from drug abuse," according to the artful Art. Diane is buried in Forest Lawn Memorial Park in the Hollywood Hills. Her simple plaque reads DARLING, WE LOVED YOU SO MUCH.

AH, love. In 1962, legendary costume designer Irene (1907–1962) confided in her pal Doris Day that she was still madly in love with actor Gary Cooper, even though Coop had died a year earlier. On November 15, three weeks short of her sixty-second birthday, Irene checked into Los Angeles's Knickerbocker Hotel under an assumed name. She drank quite a bit of booze then cut her wrists, but when she realized she didn't cut deep enough to bleed to death, she jumped out the bathroom window of her eleventh-floor suite. It was a little after 3 p.m., and Irene landed on the extended roof of the lobby. She wasn't discovered until later that night. She had left notes for friends and family (In part, her suicide note read: "I'm sorry; this is the best way. Take care of the business and get someone very good to design. Love to all. Irene."), and for the hotel residents, apologizing for any inconvenience her death caused

("Neighbors: Sorry I had to drink so much to get the courage to do this.").

Flushed with Excitement

CAROLE Landis (1919–1948) was known as "the Chest" thanks to her 36DD rack. And the rest of her wasn't bad either. The actress entertained troops during World War II; her 1945 trip almost killed her when she contracted amoebic dysentery and malaria. That same year, Landis starred on Broadway in the musical *A Lady Says Yes*, and the lady did say yes, to an affair with costar Jacqueline Susann, who, years later, would use Landis as the basis for the neurotic Jennifer North in her odious opus *Valley of the Dolls*. Yet even that novel couldn't compare to the juicy scandal in Carole's real life. She had been plagued by depression her entire life and tried to kill herself in 1944 and 1946. In 1948, with a career that was fading and a marriage that was ending, the twenty-nine-year-old actress finally committed suicide by taking an overdose of Seconal. Her body was discovered by actor Rex Harrison, with whom she was having an affair and with whom she dined the previous night. Harrison was the last person to see Landis alive . . . and the first to see her dead, on the bathroom floor. He'd claim he felt a pulse, yet instead of summoning an ambulance, he left the house; by the time he returned, Landis had been dead for hours.

Landis left two suicide notes. The one to her mother read, "Dearest Mommie, I'm sorry, really sorry, to put you through this but there is no way to avoid it. I love you darling, you have been the most wonderful mom ever. And that applies to all our family. I love each and every one of them dearly. Everything goes to you—look in the files and there is a will which decrees everything. Good bye, my angel. Pray for me, Your Baby." The second note was addressed to Harrison, who bribed a police officer to destroy it.

Landis is buried wearing her favorite blue dress with orchids on the shoulder straps and a gold cross pendant, at curbside in the Everlasting Love section of Forest Lawn Memorial Park in Glendale. Carole's mother and sister never believed that Landis committed suicide and tried for years to connect Harrison with the death. They never succeeded.

MEXICAN-BORN María Guadalupe Villalobos Vélez, better known as Lupe Velez (1908–1944), may have been the former wife of Johnny "Tarzan" Weissmuller and the love slave of Gary Cooper, but it was her date with a john that keeps her name alive. Cynics insist Velez died in bed, but this is Hollyweird, where facts are so easily flushed away. The Mexican Spitfire left this cruel world, pregnant by her married lover, Austrian actor Harald Maresch, by drowning herself . . . in her toilet. She was thirty-six. It was to be an exit forever remembered. Lupe had her hair and nails done. She filled her bedroom with flowers and surrounded her bed with lighted candles. After taking pills, she arranged herself on the bed so it would look like she was sleeping peacefully. She was wearing blue satin pajamas. The suicide note was succinct: "To Harald, May God forgive you and forgive me too but I prefer to take my life away and our baby's before I bring him with shame or killing him, Lupe."

But the drugs didn't go well with her lunch of burritos and enchiladas, so she staggered to her orchid-color bathroom, slipped on the tile, and plunged head first into the commode. Her devoted secretary discovered her wet and stiff body the next day. Velez's funeral was held at Forest

Lawn in Glendale; her remains and those of her unborn baby were laid to rest in the Rotonda de las Personas Ilustres in Mexico City.

Too Tough to Swallow

HERS was a most colorful life. The first husband of Swedish blue-eyed Inger Stevens (1934–1970) was her agent, Anthony Soglio; from 1961 to her death, she was secretly married to black actor Ike Jones. Then, of course, there were starry-eyed flings with the likes of Anthony Quinn, Bing Crosby, Mario Lanza, and Burt Reynolds. See, gentlemen really do prefer blondes.

A houseguest found Inger lying facedown on her kitchen floor on the morning of April 30. She called the actress's name; Inger opened her eyes and let out a muffled groan then lapsed into unconsciousness. An ambulance rushed her to the hospital, but she was pronounced dead at 10:30 a.m. Dr. Thomas Noguchi concluded that Stevens died from "acute barbiturate intoxication due to ingestion of overdose," though a recent chin cut remained unexplained. Police, however, said that Stevens had died from swallowing "a caustic substance, possibly cleaning fluid." It was later rumored to be a bottle of ammonia. Talk about cleaning out your pipes!

But Stevens's death, at age thirty-five, is shrouded in mystery. Why would an actress who had a hit with the series *The Farmer's Daughter* and was about to begin production on a new Aaron Spelling TV series (ironically titled *The Most Deadly Game*) snuff out her life? Accidental overdose? Suicide? Or murder? Although it was later revealed that Stevens had previously attempted suicide on January 1, 1960 (she was discovered by a janitor who broke into her apartment at the request of a TV executive worried that he hadn't heard from her) the secret to her second and final attempt went right to her grave—she was cremated and her ashes sprinkled over the Pacific Ocean.

POLISH-BORN actress Bella Darvi (1928–1971) survived a World War II concentration camp and suicide attempts in 1962, 1966, and 1968. She finally succeeded on September 10, in her Monte Carlo apartment. Her body, unfortunately, wasn't found until a week after she turned on the gas oven. Darvi killed herself on the same day that Italian beauty and one-time James Dean "girlfriend" Pier Angeli (1932–1971) swallowed a fatal overdose of barbiturates.

BRITISH cryptographer, mathematician, philosopher, and very much the father of modern-date computers Alan Turing (1912–1954) was gay at a time when homosexuality was illegal in the United Kingdom and subject to criminal sanctions. Turing was charged with gross indecency; to avoid imprisonment, he agreed to undergo hormonal treatment. On June 7, the math whiz died of cyanide poisoning—he had laced an apple (found half eaten near his body) with the poison, reenacting a scene from "Snow White," his favorite fairy tale.

THE older sister of actress Mariel Hemingway and the granddaughter of writer Ernest Hemingway, model/actress Margaux Hemingway (1955–1996) ended it all on July 1— one day before the thirty-fifth anniversary of her grandfather's own suicide. Margaux took an overdose of phenobarbital and was found in her Santa Monica, California, apartment. She was lying on the bed, her legs propped up on a pillow, a book in her lap. Three vials of the barbiturate Klonopin were found in her apartment; two were empty and one still contained five tablets. Hemingway, whose battles with bulimia and alcoholism generated more ink than her film career, did not have a prescription for the drug. She was cremated, and buried in the Hemingway family plot in the Ketchum Cemetery in Ketchum, Idaho.

THE name Florence Lawrence (1886–1938) may not have a familiar ring these days, but back in the early days of motion pictures she was so famous that she's considered Hollywood's First Movie Star—the first actress known to the public by name. In 1915, after making countless films, she was seriously injured while shooting a stunt and later, seriously burned when a staged fire got out of control. (Imagine her horror when she learned that the studio would not pay her medical bills!) Her body and spirit wracked in pain, Lawrence's star began to fade. Though she later would be hired by MGM for bit roles at an insulting $75 per week rate, Lawrence died without ever making a comeback. Hollywood wouldn't cough it up, so on December 27, Lawrence mixed together cough syrup and ant poison. It was her last meal. She is buried in Hollywood Forever in Hollywood, California, with an incorrect birth year of 1890 on her tombstone.

A Blazing Finale

BLOND, blue-eyed great Dane Gwili Andre (1908–1959) made headlines by being a Garbo look-alike, dating Howard Hughes, and being (at the time) the highest priced model in America. She also died from those headlines. On the day after her fifty-first birthday, the penniless alcoholic, angry that her movie career never ignited, surrounded herself with publicity photographs and press clippings, then set the papers on fire. Police found the actress smoldering on her bathroom floor. For one last time, Andre made the papers—all the news that's fit to kill.

Presidential Passings

FINAL EXITS OF FIRST FAMILIES

Capitol Concerns

NO American president has ever been cremated. But, to date, thirty people have lain in state or in honor at the Rotunda of the U.S. Capitol. There are no laws, rules, or regulations specifying who may be put on public view; whether or not you get the okay is determined by the agreement of the House and Senate, provided, of course, permission is granted by survivors and the person "has rendered distinguished service to the nation." Civil rights pioneer Rosa Parks (1913–2005) made history again when she became the first woman ever to lie in honor in the Capitol Rotunda (October 30–31, 2005).

Every casket sits on the same catafalque, which was hastily constructed in 1865 to support the casket of Abraham Lincoln. Although the simple bier of rough pine boards nailed together and covered with black cloth is basically the same as it was in Lincoln's time, its base and platform have been altered to accommodate larger coffins. When not in use, the catafalque is stored in the small vaulted chamber known as Washington's Tomb, the original, but never used, resting spot of our first president.

Some of those who shared the catafalque and the dates they were lying around:

Unknown Soldiers of World War II and the Korean War (May 28–30, 1958)

John Fitzgerald Kennedy (November 24–25, 1963)

Douglas MacArthur (April 8–9, 1964)

J. Edgar Hoover (May 3–4, 1972)

Unknown Soldier of Vietnam Era (May 25–28, 1984)

Ronald Wilson Reagan (June 9–11, 2004)

Gerald R. Ford Jr. (December 30, 2006–January 2, 2007)

Next Time, We Take Amtrak

THE "Lincoln Train," the locomotive carrying the body of Abraham Lincoln (1809–1865), visited so many towns as its retraced Abe's historical path to the White House that when the body finally arrived in Springfield, Illinois, an undertaker was forced to use white chalk to conceal the damage to the corpse's face. Lincoln's massive sarcophagus in Springfield, Illinois's Oak Ridge Cemetery is empty—the president is buried in the ground ten feet below it. In 1876, thieves and counterfeiters broke into his tomb, planning to hold the body for a $200,000 ransom. They were caught and sentenced to one year in jail on a charge of lock-breaking. Since there was no law against grave robbing, the state legislature quickly passed a bill.

Short on Term

WILLIAM Henry Harrison (1773–1841), the ninth president of the United States, gave the longest inaugural address in history—it ran 8,444 words, and took about one hour and forty-five minutes to utter, even though his friend Daniel Webster had edited it for length. Though it was drizzling and quite cold that March 4 day, Harrison insisted on not wearing a hat or topcoat. And so he caught pneumonia, dying a month later. He served thirty-one days in office.

History Repeating Itself

JOHN Adams (1735–1826) and Thomas Jefferson (1743–1826) both died within hours of each other on July 4. Adams's final words? "Thomas Jefferson survives." But he was wrong: TJ had died a few hours earlier. Jefferson designed his own tombstone and specifically requested that his jobs as vice president and president not be mentioned. Five years to the date, on July 4, 1831, fifth president James Monroe (1758–1831) found his afterlife independence. If fourth president James Madison (1751–1836) had held on a week longer, he could have joined the Executive Exiting Club. But he refused medication, leaving instead on June 28.

Desperate Housewife?

WHEN her husband, President Warren G. Harding (1865–1923), died First Lady Florence Harding refused an autopsy and had the body embalmed within an hour. Mystery still lingers over his death. Harding's politics have caused him to be consistently ranked as one of the worst U.S. presidents; it was a well-known fact that he had a mistress and an illegitimate child. Dead at fifty-seven from a heart attack? Maybe. Many believe he was poisoned—by his wife. While awaiting a state funeral, Harding's dead body was on display in the East Room of the White House, where employees were quoted as saying that the night before the funeral, they heard Mrs. Harding speak for more than an hour to her dead husband.

The Last Daze of Camelot

JOHN F. Kennedy (1917–1963) never made it to his 1 p.m. lunch appointment in Dallas—he was assassinated just thirty minutes earlier as his motorcade entered Delaney Plaza. But at least he went out on a full stomach. On the morning of November 22, 1963, Kennedy was served coffee, orange juice, two eggs (soft-boiled at five minutes), and toast with marmalade on the side. The food was prepared and served by Otto Druhe, the executive chef at the Hilton Fort Worth, the hotel JFK and First Lady Jacqueline were staying at before leaving the next morning for Dallas. Kennedy's last meal (and final speech) took place in the Crystal Ballroom, where two thousand supporters joined them for breakfast. (The room has since been remodeled and renumbered; ask real nicely and the staff will tell you which one it is.)

Kennedy's death continues to be shrouded in mystery, but a few facts are etched in stone. Even though Kennedy was DOA at Parkland Memorial Hospital, he was "officially" pronounced dead at 1:33 p.m. after the Very Rev. Oscar L. Huber gave him the last rites. Huber recalls that he had to "draw back a sheet covering the President's face" in order to do his duty. Secret Service agent Clint Hill, riding on the left front running board of the car immediately behind the president's, recalls that former first lady Jacqueline tried to climb onto the actual rear of the limo, perhaps trying to retrieve a fragment of her hubby's shattered skill.

And though Jackie Kennedy (1929–1994) swore under oath she did not remember such a moment, she did take some secrets to her husband's grave. After the assassination, she wrote her late hubby a letter, and asked their two children to do the same. Jackie took the three letters, a pair of gold-enameled cufflinks she had given him as a wedding gift, and a piece of scrimshaw carved with the presidential seal that she had given him for Christmas and tossed them in his coffin. Brother Robert F. Kennedy threw in a PT-109 tie-clip and a silver rosary.

Real Reality TV

AT 11:21 on the morning of November 24, 1963, just two days after he was arrested for the assassination of President John F. Kennedy, Lee Harvey Oswald (1939–1963) was shot and fatally wounded on live television. His assassin was Dallas nightclub owner Jack Ruby, who claimed he committed the crime because he was "distraught" over Kennedy's killing. Oswald was rushed to Parkland Memorial Hospital, the same hospital where Kennedy had died. Doctors attempted to save Oswald's life, but the lone bullet had severed major abdominal blood vessels beyond repair. Exactly forty-eight hours and seven minutes after JFK's death, Oswald was pronounced dead at 1:07 p.m.

On October 4, 1981, Oswald's body was exhumed at the request of a British writer who wanted to prove that the man buried was not Oswald but a Russian spy who had stolen Oswald's identity in Russia—and thus was the real killer of JFK. With Oswald's widow's support, the grave was opened. His simple moleskin-covered pine coffin had rotted and was filled with water, and what remains remained were so badly decomposed that positive identification of the corpse was made through Oswald's dental records. A childhood mastoid scar offered a secondary confirmation.

Oswald was reburied in the same spot, in a new casket containing a few fragments of the old one. There was stiff bidding at the auction of the mortuary toe tag from Oswald's corpse—when the gavel fell at a 2008 Manhattan auction, the tag sold for $66,000. (The tag had bloodstains and a lock of Oswald's hair tied to it with white thread.)

Bushwhacked!

LET'S not beat around the bush. On the evening of November 6, 1963, two days after she turned seventeen, future first lady Laura Welch killed a man. She was out celebrating her birthday, and failed to stop her Chevy Impala sedan at a stop sign, smashing into a Corvair being driven by high school football star Michael Dutton Douglas (1945–1963). Laura and her passenger, Judy Dykes, were treated for minor injuries at nearby Midland Memorial Hospital; that's where they learned that Douglas was DOA, dead from a broken neck. No charges were filed. In May 2000, a two-page police report detailing the fatal crash was made public but it shed no further light on the accident. (The speed of the death mobile is illegible on the report.) The first lady, who many say was romantically linked with Douglas, says nothing about that night, though in 2000, her spokesman Andrew Malcolm uttered, "To this day Mrs. Bush remains unable to talk about it." Douglas is buried in Austin Memorial Park Cemetery in Austin, Texas. No bushes are in sight.

Out in the Open?

JAMES Buchanan (1791–1868) was the only president never to have married. Many people think he was gay, but he had one serious romantic link, with a woman named Anne Coleman. She died unexpectedly in 1819, shortly after the couple quarreled, leaving the suicidal president to muse that his happiness would "be buried with her in the grave." Two days before Buchanan died, he left specific instructions that a letter explaining why the couple split and never married be burned . . . without ever being opened.

Criminal Intent

LAW AND DISORDER

Into the Woods

CHARLES Lindbergh Jr. (1930–1932), the first child of the famed aviator and his wife, Anne Morrow, was kidnapped from the second-floor bedroom of the Lindbergh's Hopewell, New Jersey, home between 8 and 10 p.m. on March 1, 1932. A wooden ladder was found leaning against the house; an envelope left on the windowsill contained a crudely written ransom note demanding $50,000 for the safe return of the baby. A second note anted up the ransom to $70,000 and scolded Lindbergh for calling the police. On April 2, a Lindbergh pal acted as a go-between, delivering the seventy grand in marked gold certificates to the unknown kidnapper. The note he received in return indicated where Charlie Jr. could be found. He was not there.

The baby was finally found on May 12, in woods just four miles from the Lindbergh estate. His skull had a massive fracture; the fatal blow had been delivered the night of the kidnapping. On September 15, 1934, carpenter Bruno Richard Hauptmann (1899–1936) bought gasoline with one of the marked bills. Thinking the bill counterfeit, the attendant wrote down the car's license plate number. Police found $14,000 of the ransom money in Hauptmann's garage and arrested him. Hauptmann insisted he was framed, yet evidence—including a rafter from his house's attic matching a timber used to make the ladder and ransom note writing that matched his handwriting—proved otherwise. The country's "Trial of the Century" convicted the illegal immigrant of kidnapping and murder, and Hauptmann was sent to the electric chair on April 3.

The Lindbergh baby was cremated, his ashes scattered over the Atlantic. Hauptmann was also cremated. No one knows what happened to his ashes.

When Fans Turn Wild

ROBERT John Bardo, a nineteen-year-old who had previously stalked Tiffany and Madonna, paid $250 to a Tucson detective agency to get the home address of Rebecca Lucile Schaeffer (1967–1989). Then he paid a call to the star of *My Sister Sam*. On July 18, he shot her at point-blank range using a handgun procured by his brother. A neighbor heard her screams and found her body, clad in a black robe, twitching in the building's foyer, although she had no pulse. Bardo was tried by prosecutor Marcia Clark, later to become famous for her role in the O. J. Simpson trial, and convicted of capital murder. He is serving life in prison without the possibility of parole. Schaeffer's murder prompted the state of California to pass antistalking laws.

||||||||||||||||||||||||||||||||||||||||||||||||||||||||||||||||||||||||||||||||||||||||||||||||||||||||||||||||||||||||

Just the facts, ma'am: Jack Webb (1920–1982) was buried with full police honors (including a seventeen-gun salute), although the *Dragnet* star had never actually served on the force. Los Angeles police chief Darryl Gates also made the arresting news that badge no. 714, used by Webb's character Joe Friday in the crime series, would be officially laid to rest as well.   💀

||||||||||||||||||||||||||||||||||||||||||||||||||||||||||||||||||||||||||||||||||||||||||||||||||||||||||||||||||||||

A Stranglehold on the Truth

SHE was neither rich nor famous, nor a movie star, though she certainly was pretty enough to pass as one. Yet sweet-natured Mary Sullivan (1944–1964) became a celebrity at nineteen, when she became the last victim of the Boston Strangler, one of America's first modern-day serial killers. Mary was found in her Charles Street apartment on January 4, sprawled out and sexually abused and strangled just like eleven other victims. (Today, Mary's former apartment is a popular spot on Beantown sightseeing tours.) Laborer Albert DeSalvo (1931–1973) admitted to being the Strangler, and although he was sentenced to life in prison after being convicted in other rape cases, he was never legally convicted of the strangling crimes, leaving them still officially listed as "unsolved." In November 1973, DeSalvo was stabbed six times in the heart by a fellow inmate at the Walpole State Prison during a prison brawl. His killer was never identified.

In 2001, Sullivan's place in macabre memorial history was changed. With the blessings of both the Sullivan and DeSalvo families, Sullivan's remains were disinterred from her Cape Cod grave and De Salvo was taken from his Peabody burial spot. A twelve-member team of forensic experts then broke the news, faster than a neck could snap: Despite DeSalvo's insistence that he sexually assaulted Sullivan, the findings concluded that "DNA on Miss Sullivan's pubic hair appeared to come from a semen stain and did not match DNA from Mr. DeSalvo." Show over, Sullivan was once again buried in her plot at Saint Francis Xavier Cemetery in Centerville and De Salvo went back to Puritan Lawn Memorial Park.

Dickering Around with Death

IS it true that when John Dillinger (1903–1934) was ambushed and gunned down, it was revealed that he had an eighteen-inch penis? As we celebrate the seventy-fifth anniversary of Dillinger's death, the rumor unzips. America's most famous Public Enemy No. 1 (the first time such a designation was used by the FBI) was gunned down in an alley outside the Biograph Theater in Chicago. He, gal pal Polly Hamilton, and Polly's friend Anna Sage had just seen *Manhattan Melodrama*. What John and Polly didn't know was that Sage was a madam whose deportation hearings had already begun, and she'd made a deal with the FBI: She'd lead them to their man; they'd stop her deportation. As they exited the theater, Sage tipped off FBI agents, who opened fire on Dillinger. He was struck three times—twice in the chest, one nicking his heart, and the fatal shot, which entered the back of his neck and exited just under his right eye. He was pronounced dead at 10:50 p.m. on July 22 at Alexian Brothers Hospital and buried at Crown Hill Cemetery in Indianapolis. His gravestone is often vandalized by people seeking souvenirs. Please don't get any ideas: A three-foot slab of reinforced concrete has since been poured over the grave to discourage would-be robbers.

But the schlong story survives. Dillinger's morgue shot shows what looks like a shockingly oversized erection. The rumor was that Dillinger was so well-endowed that his penis was removed, preserved, and secretly sent to the Smithsonian Institution. Not true. The "erection" was the awkward angle of his arm, stiff from rigor mortis. To this day, the Smithsonian receives scores of calls each year from the morbidly curious asking if the story is true. You can now be cocksure it ain't.

Crime does pay: Each July 22, the John Dillinger Died for You Society observes "John Dillinger Day," where crime buffs, the curious, and the wacky gather at Chicago's Biograph Theater on the anniversary of the criminal's death. A bagpiper (playing "Amazing Grace") leads revelers on the path to retrace Dillinger's fatal run into the alley where he died. Afterward, the party gathers at a restaurant across the street from the theater for refreshments.

‖‖

Lizzie Borden took an axe
And gave her mother forty whacks.
And when she saw what she had done
She gave her father forty-one.

The famous jump-rope rhyme is wrong: Mama Abby was hacked a mere nineteen times, Daddy got ten whacks. Lizzie was acquitted of the 1892 crime and died at sixty-six. ☻

‖‖

Seeing Reds

AMERICAN industrialist Henry Clay Frick (1849–1919) was often called "America's Most Hated Man" because of his strong antiworker and antiunion stances. Those stances shot into the spotlight on July 6, 1892, when striking steelworkers of the works at Homestead, together with citizens of the town, were confronted by an army of Pinkerton agents hired by Frick. There was so much violence and fire and bloodshed that Pennsylvania's governor placed Homestead Works under martial law. Today, the Homestead Strike is known as the most famous—and one of the most violent—labor disputes in U.S. history.

What goes around . . . on July 23, 1892, anarchist Alexander Berkman (1880–1936) sought revenge. Armed with a revolver and a sharp steel file, he entered Frick's Pittsburgh office. Frick rose from his chair just as Berkman pulled the gun and fired at nearly point-blank range. The bullet hit his left earlobe, penetrated his neck near the base of the skull, and lodged in his back. Frick was hurled across the room while Berkman fired again, this time striking Frick again in the neck. Blood rushed as freely as the Allegheny. Still no dead Frick. Berkman then stabbed Frick four times in the leg with the file before being subdued and dragged away by employees. Police entered with guns drawn, but Frick cried, "Don't shoot! Leave him to the law, but raise his head and let me see his face." Frick was as tough as the steel whose profits made him rich. Doctors probed his body for two hours looking for the bullets; Frick refused anesthesia so he could help guide their efforts. He was back to work in a week. Berkman was charged and found guilty of attempted murder. He was sentenced to twenty-two years in prison and eventually served fourteen before, under pressure from labor union supporters, he was pardoned in 1906.

Frick finally died, of a heart attack, on December 2, just weeks before his seventieth birthday. On the night Frick's flame flickered out, Berkman and fellow anarchist Emma Goldman (1869–1940) were in Chicago attending a banquet, their last public appearance before being tossed out of the country by feds. A newsman approached Berkman with news of Frick's death. His reaction? "Frick had been deported by God. I'm glad he left the country before me."

Berkman, suffering from prostate cancer, eventually committed suicide. What another mess he made! The bullet didn't do its job, lodging in his spinal column and paralyzing him. Goldman rushed to his side just before he sank into a coma. Berkman died at ten that night.

In 1940, Goldman died in Toronto, Canada, of a stroke.

Her body was allowed to be returned to the United States and she is buried in Chicago's German Waldheim Cemetery. Her gravestone bears the incorrect death date of 1939. If she had hung around until 1981, she would have witnessed Maureen Stapleton win a Best Actress Oscar for her portrayal of Goldman in the film *Reds*.

An Eye for Murder

IF you're going to get wiped out by the mob, you might as well be comfortable, at your girlfriend's swanky Beverly Hills home, relaxing on a nice plush sofa. Benjamin "Bugsy" Siegel (1906–1947) would have agreed. On that June night not so long ago, as the lady-killer was reading the newspaper, a spray of bullets from a .30-caliber military M1 carbine was fired through a window. No one was charged with the murder, and the crime remains officially unsolved, though everyone believes ex-mobster Eddie Cannizzaro entered the backyard and did the deadly deed. If so, he was a good shot. But even though the autopsy revealed that one bullet entered the back of Bugsy's skull, exiting through an eye (police later found the eyeball across the room), the actual cause of death was a cerebral hemorrhage. Four of the nine shots fired that night destroyed a white marble statue of Bacchus on a grand piano, and then lodged in the far wall. Morgue photos of the gangster show cotton balls where his eyes once were.

Down and Flat-Out in L.A.

CHANGING a flat tire alone late at night or early in the morning may not be a smart move. That's why they invented the Automobile Association of America. At about 1 a.m. on January 16, Ennis Cosby (1969–1997), the only son of funny man Bill, was approaching the Skirball Center

Drive of Interstate 405 in the hills above Brentwood when he realized the front left tire of the $130,000 green Mercedes 600SL convertible registered to his father's company had a flat tire. He used his cell to call the female friend he was on his way to visit; she lived less than ten minutes away and drove to meet Cosby. Arriving just a few minutes later, she parked her black Jaguar next to his car so that her headlights could guide him as he changed the flat. As Ennis finished fixing the tire, a man holding a gun suddenly tapped on her window and threatened to kill her. She sped away but returned at 1:28 a.m. to find Ennis lying in a pool of blood.

Members of the Los Angeles Police Department broke the news to Ennis's dad on the set of his TV series; they recalled him muttering, "I just can't believe it" repeatedly. Bill Cosby would later offer, through a plea published in the *National Enquirer*, a $100,000 reward for the capture of the killer. Two days later, the facts fell into place. While working on the car, Ennis had been assailed by unemployed Ukrainian teen Mikhail Markhasev, who demanded money before shooting Cosby in the head. Crime-scene photos show that Ennis's body was found faceup, a pack of Natural American Spirit cigarettes in one hand, a bullet wound in his left temple, and a split lip, indicating Markhasev also kicked him in the mouth. The photos also show gunpowder traces—Cosby was killed within a four-foot range. Markhasev was found guilty when his DNA was identified in a cap wrapped around the murder weapon.

Just as bold was Markhasev's next move: In a handwritten letter to California deputy attorney general Kyle Brodie, he apologized to the Cosby family and added, "Although my appeal is in its beginning stages, I don't want to continue with it because it's based on falsehood and deceit. I am guilty and I want to do the right thing. This is not about me, but about those whose lives I've marred. My motive is to at least try to mend the things which I've destroyed. More than anything, I want to apologize to the victim's family. It is my duty as a Christian, and it's the least I can do, after the great wickedness for which I am responsible." Ennis was buried in a private ceremony attended by sixteen family members and friends at the Cosbys' 265-acre farm in Shelburne, Massachusetts. Markhasev is serving a life sentence in Corcoran State Prison.

Double Trouble

LET us time travel, for a brief paragraph or two, to the Roaring Twenties, to the most shocking and scandalous crime of its day. Bronx housewife Ruth Snyder was bent on two things: killing her husband, Albert, and continuing her affair with corset salesman Judd Gray. Previous attempts to snuff out Albert failed—she tried twice by asphyxiation and once by poison. But she had persuaded her husband to take out a $48,000 double indemnity insurance policy . . . which would pay her in the event of his accidental death.

And so her lover got in on the act. The duo decided to murder him, then stage a burglary. When Albert came home, Ruth and Judd smashed his skull with a window sash weight, strangled him with a garrote fashioned out of picture wire and a gold pen, then stuffed chloroform-soaked rags into his nostrils.

The staged burglary, this "perfect crime," smelled funny to the police. Long before the Lindbergh baby flew the coop, decades before O.J. punted his way onto the scene, this was the Crime of the Century. The media circus lured celebrities such as director D. W. Griffith and evangelists Billy Sunday and Aimee Semple McPherson. Some found Ruth's criminal actions attractive; she received more than 150 marriage proposals. Ruth's plea for clemency would be denied. She died in Sing Sing's electric chair on January 12. Judd took a seat next.

Perhaps more shocking than the crime was at the exact moment of Ruth's death, the very moment the voltage ran through her body, photographer Tom Howard raised his pant cuff and, with the miniature camera strapped to his leg, snapped a now-infamous front-page New York *Daily News* photo. (The camera he used is part of the collections of the Smithsonian's National Museum of American History.) The headline screamed DEAD! with a hazy image of Snyder being fried. So famous is the photo that even Andy Warhol had a copy in his collection.

BONNIE Parker (1910–1934) and Clyde Barrow (1909–1934) were partners in crime, and in life. The notorious outlaws, who killed fourteen people (nine of whom were policemen) during their reign of terror, were finally ambushed in a rainstorm of bullets as they whizzed through a stretch of Louisiana highway at eighty-five miles per hour. Each died with weapons in their hands (police would later find fourteen guns and fifteen hundred rounds of ammo in the car), but they didn't get to use them. A bit after 9 a.m., six lawmen hiding in the woods riddled the Ford V-8 with bullets at such velocity that each passed through Barrow's body, then through Parker, then through the car's passenger-side door. Each corpse would have more than twenty-five bullet wounds. Bonnie was found leaning against her lover's body. They longed to be buried side by side. In fact, two years before their deaths, Parker, who fancied herself a poetess, wrote a poem about that inevitable day: "Some day they will go down together / And they will bury them side by side / To a few it means grief / To the law it's relief / But it's death to Bonnie and Clyde." Bonnie's mother Emma nixed the idea.

The morticians had a great time dressing the couple for

their farewell tour. A plastic surgeon restored the back of Barrow's head that had been blown away; you couldn't even tell an ear was missing. He wore a pin-striped gray suit with a stiff while collar. A gray tie was dotted with a pearl stickpin. The corner of a white handkerchief peeked out from a lapel pocket. Bonnie was clad in a flimsy blue nightie. Her hair had been coiffed and her fingernails manicured. Bonnie's casket was made of steel, and Emma splurged on a steel vault as well.

Following a private sunset funeral on Friday, May 25, Clyde was buried in Western Heights Cemetery in Dallas. His battleship gray wooden casket (with cream satin interior) sits next to that of his brother, Marvin; the single tombstone bears the words once chosen by Barrow: "Gone but not forgotten." More than twenty thousand people turned out for Bonnie's funeral, making it difficult for the Parkers to reach the grave site at Crown Hill Memorial Park in Dallas. Bonnie's gravestone is engraved with a poem, written by the criminal herself: "As the flowers are all made sweeter by the sunshine and the dew, so this old world is made brighter by the lives of folks like you."

ALMOST a century later people still talk about the crimes Ferdinando Nicola Sacco (1891–1927) and Bartolomeo Vanzetti (1888–1927) may or may not have committed. The Italian-born laborers and anarchists were tried, convicted, and electrocuted on August 23 for the 1920 armed robbery and murder of two men. Exactly fifty years after their execution, then-governor of Massachusetts Michael Dukakis issued a proclamation stating that Sacco and Vanzetti had been treated unjustly by not being given a fair trial. "Any stigma and disgrace should be forever removed from the names of Nicola Sacco and Bartolomeo Vanzetti," he said. "We are not here to say whether these men are guilty or innocent. We are here to say that the high standards of justice, which we in Massachusetts take such pride in, failed Sacco and Vanzetti." Dukakis was forced to later express regret for not also reaching out to the families of the victims of the crime. The pair's ashes were divided into thirds; the only third known to exist is in the possession of the Boston Public Library. The ashes of both men are "mingled together in a can," the library's PR flak says, "and are available to anyone who makes an appointment to see them." While there, you can also check out their death masks.

Wouldn't Going AWOL Have Been Better?

U.S. ARMY veteran Timothy James McVeigh (1968–2001) made history the wrong way. He bombed the Alfred P. Murrah Building in Oklahoma City on the second anniversary of the Waco Siege, an act of revenge, he would claim, against what he considered to be a tyrannical government. The bombing killed 168 people and was the deadliest act of terrorism prior to 9/11.

He offered no last words before being executed by lethal injection at 7:14 a.m. on June 11, 2001. Instead, he handed the warden a copy of William Ernest Henley's poem "Invictus" as his final statement. Congress worked quickly, passing special legislation preventing McVeigh from being buried in any military cemetery, an honor that would usually be offered to a deceased veteran. He was cremated at Mattox Ryan Funeral Home in Terre Haute, with his remains given to his lawyer, who scattered them at an undisclosed location.

A Life Cut Short

SHE was only twenty-two when she died, but today Elizabeth Short (1924–1947) is best remembered by those who only know her from her nickname, the "Black Dahlia," conceived by newspaper reporters covering her grisly murder.

On January 15, 1947, housewife Betty Bersinger and her three-year-old daughter left their home in the Leimert Park section of Los Angeles on their way to a shoe repair shop. Betty felt a bit depressed as she reached the corner of Norton and 39th but shrugged it off, attributing her emotional state to the gray skies and the cold, dreary morning.

Then Betty caught a glimpse of something white in the weeds.

At first she thought it yet another piece of litter. But why would someone toss out a broken department store mannequin? The dummy had split in half and the pieces lay separate from one another. Betty and her child continued walking, occasionally glancing back. Then it hit her: She was looking at the severed body of a woman. She grabbed her daughter, ran to a nearby house, and called the police. The body was severely mutilated, drained of blood, and had the organs removed. Her face was slashed from the corners of her mouth toward her ears, a practice known by the nickname "the Glasgow Smile."

Short's life was hardly full of smiles. Born in Hyde Park, Massachusetts, she lived with her mother. Troubled by asthma, she spent winters in Florida; at the age of nineteen, she went to live with her father in California, where she worked as a waitress and a hooker. She was arrested on September 23, 1943, for underage drinking and was sent back east by juvenile authorities. She eventually wound up back in Los Angeles . . . but not in one piece.

Short's death unleashed the largest investigation by the Los Angeles Police Department since 1927. Everyone who knew (and didn't know) her was suspect. The public, fueled by lurid headlines, gruesome photos, and meticulous details of the carnage, ate up the case. Some sixty people confessed to the murder—mostly men, as well as a few women. Today, decades after the murder, the case remains unsolved, though several people have come forth, writing books, even "naming" the killer.

A widely circulated rumor holds that Short was unable to have sexual intercourse because of a genetic defect that left her with "infantile genitalia." Los Angeles County district attorney's files state investigators questioned three men with whom Short had sex. According to the Los Angeles Police Department's summary of the case, the autopsy describes Short's reproductive organs as anatomically normal.

LAST MEALS

Everybody's gotta eat. Here are the last meals of some of death row's most infamous residents. Why watch calories now?

• Pretty boy serial killer Ted Bundy, electrocuted on January 24, 1989: Steak (medium rare), eggs (over easy), hash browns, buttered toast, orange juice, and coffee.

• Nazi war criminal Adolf Eichmann, hanged May 31, 1962: Half a bottle of Carmel (a dry red Israeli wine).

• Serial killer John Wayne Gacy, executed by lethal injection on May 10, 1994: A dozen deep-fried shrimp, a bucket of Original Recipe Kentucky Fried Chicken, french fries, a pound of strawberries, and Diet Coke.

• Murderer Gary Gilmore, shot by firing squad on January 17, 1977: A hamburger, hard-boiled eggs, a baked potato, coffee, and three shots of whiskey.

• Kidnapper/murderer Bruno Richard Hauptmann, electrocuted on April 3, 1936: Celery, olives, chicken, french fries, buttered peas, cherries, and a slice of cake.

• Heretic Joan of Arc, burned at the stake on May 30, 1431: Holy Communion.

• Oklahoma City bomber Timothy McVeigh, executed by lethal injection on June 11, 2001: Two pints of mint chocolate chip ice cream.

• *In Cold Blood* killers Perry Smith and Richard Hickock, hanged on April 14, 1965: Shrimp, french fries, garlic bread, ice cream, strawberries, and whipped cream.

• Thrill killers Ruth Snyder and Judd Gray, electrocuted on January 12, 1928: Gray had chicken soup, chicken, mashed potatoes, celery, stuffed olives, and ice cream, followed by a cigar. Snyder nibbled on the hope she'd get a last-minute reprieve.

• Serial killer Aileen Wuornos, executed by lethal injection on October 9, 2002: A hamburger, snack food, and a cup of coffee.

Planning Ahead

THEIR TIME HAS NOT COME (YET)

THERE'S more than a ghost of a chance fellow cryptonites will hear a symphony when Diana Ross (1944) hits her final note. She will be buried in Detroit's supreme Woodlawn Cemetery with the rest of her family. Ross's heart seems to be less gold-plated than some of her records: When original Supreme member Florence Ballard (1943–1976) died of cardiac arrest, Ross all but dismissed the tragedy: "She had it all and she threw it away. She quit the Supremes, the Supremes didn't quit her. I'm not dead. She did this to herself."

ARETHA Franklin (1942) will also be buried at Detroit's Woodlawn Cemetery, giving fans even more chances to pay her some "R-E-S-P-E-C-T."

GROUNDBREAKING gossip guru Rona Barrett (1936) wants the world to remember her personal and professional lives. Her epitaph, she says, will read: "Here lies a woman who married two men, both of whom she loved deeply. She was always known as 'Miss Rona' and ended her broadcasts with 'Keep Thinking the Good Thoughts.' This was Rona Barrett from Hollywood."

HIS wife Natalie Wood (1938–1981) has floated off to eternity, but former hubby Robert Wagner (1930) won't be anywhere near her when he kicks the bucket. The actor distinctly remembers buying a double plot at Westwood Memorial Park, where he buried Natalie after her drowning, but the cemetery claimed they lost the records. "Years later they offered to exhume Natalie and move her to another spot where we could be buried together but I didn't want to do that," he says. When his time comes, Wagner will be buried in a nineteenth-century cemetery in Aspen, Colorado. "As soon as someone is laid to rest," he muses, "the land is allowed to return to its natural state. It's absolutely pure and totally peaceful."

LONG after he's ensconced in the Great Mansion in the Sky, Hugh Hefner (1926) plans on some heavenly delights. He owns the crypt to the left of Marilyn Monroe, his first *Playboy* Playmate.

SHE'S received as much ink for her ill health as she has for her films and her love affairs. When violet-eyed legend Dame Elizabeth Rosemond Taylor (1932)—Liz to you and me and zillions of fans worldwide—is laid to rest, it will be next to her parents Francis and Sara Taylor, along the bottom row in Westwood Memorial Park's Sanctuary of Peace.

EVERYONE'S favorite virgin, Doris Day (1922), still cannot talk about the death of Rock Hudson (1925–1985) from AIDS without crying. But such pillow talk doesn't stop Day from accepting the fact we are all going into the night:

"Everyone's gonna go sometime, so I don't think all this mourning is necessary." Que sera, sera.

MENTION death to that original Cosmo girl, Helen Gurley Brown (1922)—she was editor-in-chief of the magazine for an unprecedented thirty-two years—and the beast comes out. "I do not believe in an afterlife. We are, after all, animals. Do all tigers, monkeys, Dalmatians, cougars, muskrats and Siamese cats go to heaven? Do they all come back? I suppose it's possible, but I am not religious, so this flower is going to drop off, faint and die. That's what's going to happen to me. Some day."

DYNASTY diva Joan Collins (1933) confesses that she believes "everybody thinks about death. We think about it from the first moment we're aware of it. But I am trying to prevent it as long as I can by living."

ANOTHER Dynasty diva, Diahann Carroll (1935), freely admits her preferred way to go: "I love sex. The exchange between male and female is very important. I hope to die doing it."

THOUGH he's been battling Parkinson's since 1991, Michael J. Fox (1961) is grateful that his strong family ties have kept him sane . . . and alive. "I never wanted to end up like John Belushi," he says. "I never wanted to think, 'Wow! I've got it all,' and end up in the ground."

BEING best known as a game show host may be a pain in the ass, but in the end, there are some wisecracks worth remembering. The Newlywed Game emcee Bob Eubanks (1938) recalls asking a contestant about the weirdest place she and her husband ever "made whoopee," and her response gave him what he laughs should be his epitaph: "Up the ass, Bob."

LIFE hasn't always been a cabaret for Liza Minnelli (1946), but she's finally battled the booze and remains active in AA. What she would want to see as her epitaph? "Stop groaning. Stop moaning. Stop bragging. Take the mistakes from the past and shape the future. And live one day at a time. You have a choice to make: Live or die."

Who's Suffered from Premature Obit Syndrome?

A selected few, all of whom are (as of press time) alive and well, still kicking and still ticking off the Grim Reaper:

AUTHOR and prankster Alan Abel (1930) so wanted to get into the *New York Times* that he faked his own death. According to the paper, he died of a heart attack while skiing in Utah. The paper is a bit more careful these days . . . especially when it comes to press releases including the name "Alan Abel."

ACTRESS Nancy Allen (1950) was reported to have died of a cerebral hemorrhage in Florida on October 12, 2006. On the Internet Movie Database website (www.imdb.com), her manager set the record straight: "She is NOT dead. I am her manager. I just spoke with her and thankfully, this is a rumor."

FORMER president George H.W. Bush (1924) became ill with gastroenteritis on a visit to Japan, vomited on the Japanese prime minister and collapsed. Just as his death was being announced on the *CBS Evening News*, someone realized the error and hollered for the anchor to stop.

* * *

WHILE undergoing radiation throat treatments in 1993, 007 icon Sean Connery (1930) was declared dead by Japanese and South African news agencies. The actor immediately appeared on David Letterman's show, neither shaken nor stirred.

ROCKER Alice Cooper (1948) was reported dead in an early 1970s issue of *Melody Maker*—the magazine's concert review was published in the form of a mock obituary. So many fans believed that Alice had gone to Wonderland that he issued this statement: "I'm alive, and drunk as usual."

ON September 5, 2008, Yahoo! reported that Miley Cyrus (1992) was killed when she "ran a stop sign" and "her vehicle was hit by a large truck." TMZ also reported the tall tale, then retracted it after Miley performed in concert the following night. In November 2008, someone hacked into Cyrus's YouTube account and posted a video stating she died after being hit by a drunk driver.

THE 2006 online obituary of comedian Will Ferrell (1967) began: "Actor Will Ferrell accidentally died in a freak paragliding accident yesterday in Torey [*sic*] Pines, Southern California. The accident apparently happened somewhere near the famed paragliding site after a freak wind gust basically blew Ferrell and his companion towards a wooded area where they lost control before crashing into the dense foliage . . . As horrified witnesses looked on, the duo headed straight for the dense woods near the jump off point and crashed at an estimated 60 mph hitting the trees as they hurtled to the ground."

Another hoax. Ferrell has never been paragliding.

* * *

IN 1998, James Earl Jones (1931) was mistakenly pronounced dead during a radio broadcast of a Pittsburgh Pirates baseball game by play-by-play announcer Lanny Frattare, who really struck out by confusing the actor with the assassin of Martin Luther King Jr., James Earl Ray, who had just perished.

THE "death" of singer and actress Lena Horne (1917) was posted on the online edition of *Entertainment Weekly* in 2008, with a promise that more information on her demise "is forthcoming." The obit is what is called "prewritten" because it has blanks, in this case "TK," a proofreading symbol that means "to come." The obit read: "Lena Horne, the torch singer/actress whose recording career spanned 70 years, and who sought to break Hollywood color barriers to become the screen's first African-American glamour goddess, died today at age TK in location TK from cause TK."

HI, June. How's the Beaver? Dead? Jerry Mathers (1948), who rocketed to fame on *Leave It to Beaver*, was reportedly killed in Vietnam in 1968. The urban legend began when a soldier named Private J. Mathers was killed, and news agencies confused the two. Eddie Haskell had nothing to do with this one.

AMERICA'S got talent, and networks make mistakes as easy as ABC. In 2004, the network's news department ran an incomplete obituary of Sharon Osbourne (1952) after an archived template being transferred to a new computer system went live. The obituary contained lots of information that would be filled in later—thus the Xs, here not representing kisses. It began: "Sharon Osbourne, best known as the woman who saved Ozzy Osbourne from himself, XXX

today of XXX. She was XX." ABC later apologized, insisting "It was a regrettable mistake."

BRITNEY Spears (1981) and former beau Justin Timberlake
(1981) were reported to have died in a 2001 car crash by
two DJs at a Texas radio station. The station was sued and
the DJs were fired, but not before the "news," fueled by the
Internet, was reported on international TV.

THINK of the PR value! When a 1982 *People* magazine story
referred to Abe Vigoda (1921) as "the late Abe Vigoda," the
actor proved them wrong by posing for a photograph sitting up in a coffin, holding a copy of the erroneous magazine article.

Dear World

A SELECTION OF SUICIDE NOTES

CLARA BLANDICK (1880–1962)

I am now about to make the great adventure. I cannot endure this agonizing pain any longer. It is all over my body. Neither can I face the impending blindness. I pray the Lord my soul to take. Amen.

SHE was all dressed up with somewhere to go. And it wasn't going to be Kansas. The role of Auntie Em in *The Wizard of Oz* cemented Blandick in film history, yet even the great and powerful Oz couldn't stop the eighty-one-year-old character actress from the journey she was bent on taking on April 14—not into Emerald City but to the Pearly Gates. The woman who played headstrong big-screen roles hadn't been able to live with the pain of arthritis that wracked her body; the medical news that she was going blind sent her into a deep depression.

First she went to Palm Sunday Mass. Then she wrote the farewell note. Then she fussed with her hair until it looked perfect. Dressed in a royal blue bathrobe, she lay down on the couch, covered herself with a gold-colored blanket, swallowed a handful of sleeping pills, and pulled a plastic bag over her head. Landlady Helen Mason found her body the next morning. Auntie Em was dead, blue, and slightly bloated. The official cause of death: suffocation. Police also found Blandick's resume and press clippings neatly piled on a table so that newsmen and obituary writers would get the accurate facts of her life.

KURT COBAIN (1967–1994)

. . . when we're back stage and the lights go out and the manic roar of the crowds begins, it doesn't affect me the way in which it did for Freddie Mercury, who seemed to love, relish in the love and adoration from the crowd which is something I totally admire and envy. The fact is, I can't fool you, any one of you. It simply isn't fair to you or me. The worst crime I can think of would be to rip people off by faking it and pretending as if I'm having 100% fun. Sometimes I feel as if I should have a punch-in time clock before I walk out on stage. I've tried everything within my power to appreciate it (and I do, God, believe me I do, but it's not enough). I appreciate the fact that I and we have affected and entertained a lot of people. It must be one of those narcissists who only appreciate things when they're gone. I'm too sensitive. I need to be slightly numb in order to regain the enthusiasms I once had as a child. I have a goddess of a wife who sweats ambition and empathy and a daughter who reminds me too much of what i used to be, full of love and joy, kissing every person she meets because everyone is good and will do her no harm. And that terrifies me to the point to where I can barely function. I can't stand the thought of Frances becoming the miserable, self-destructive, death rocker that I've become. I have it good, very good, and I'm grateful, but since the age of seven, I've become hateful towards all humans in general. Only because it seems so easy for people to get along that have empathy. Only because I love and feel sorry for people too much I guess.

Thank you all from the pit of my burning, nauseous stomach for your letters and concern during the past years. I'm too much of an erratic, moody baby! I don't have the passion anymore, and so remember, it's better to burn out than to fade away.

Peace, love, empathy. Frances and Courtney, I'll be at your alter. Please keep going Courtney, for Frances. For her life, which will be so much happier without me.

I LOVE YOU, I LOVE YOU!

ON April 8, 1994, the body of the lead singer of Nirvana was discovered in a garage apartment of his Seattle Lake, Washington, home by an electrician who had arrived to install a security system. He believed that Cobain was asleep until he saw the Remington 11 20-gauge shot gun pointing at his chin. High concentrations of heroin and traces of Valium were also found in his body. The coroner estimated that Cobain had been dead for at least three days.

Some people believed Cobain was murdered. The Seattle Police Department investigated, and fingerprints on the gun matched those of Cobain. After an autopsy his death was ruled a suicide by a single gunshot wound to the head, and the rocker's death certificate was stamped and sealed. The suicide note, written in red ballpoint pen, was long and rambling; the excerpt's reference to Courtney is his wife, Courtney Love; Frances is their daughter. Five days after Cobain's body was found, thousands gathered at an outdoor memorial service during which a prerecorded tape of an angry Love reading her lover's suicide note was played. She'd interrupt herself and curse Cobain, asking the fans to join her in calling him obscene names. While they listened and cussed, Love was actually attending the formal memorial service for Cobain at a nearby church. Cobain's ashes were scattered in the Wishkah River near his home in Washington and at a New York Buddhist temple. Love got the rest. Or she *had* the rest.

In 2008, Love reported that her portion of Cobain's cremains—kept in a "pink teddy bear–shaped bag along with a lock of his hair"—were stolen from her Los Angeles home. "I can't believe anyone would take Kurt's ashes from me," she said at the time. "I find it disgusting. They were all I had left of my husband. I used to take them everywhere with me just so I could feel Kurt was still with me. Now it feels like I have lost him all over again."

HART CRANE (1899–1932)

Goodbye, everybody!

MANY still feel that Crane's work is difficult beyond comprehension, but in the long run, the poet and author has proved to be one of the most influential poets of his generation. But then there's that dark side riddled with alcoholism and depression. He was gay yet fought the feeling; his only heterosexual relationship was with Peggy Cowley, the soon to be ex-wife of his friend Malcolm Cowley. On April 27, 1932, Crane was onboard the steamship *SS Orizaba*, heading back to New York from Mexico. He had just been beaten for making sexual advances at a male crewmember, and the purser locked him in his cabin, even nailing the door shut. Still, Crane got out, and just before noon, jumped into the Gulf of Mexico wearing his pajamas. His body was never recovered, but the suicide note was found inside his cabin. A marker on his father's tombstone includes the inscription, HAROLD HART CRANE 1899–1932 LOST AT SEA.

DOROTHY DANDRIDGE (1922–1965)

In case of my death—to whomever discovers it—Don't remove anything I have on—scarf, gown or underwear—Cremate me right away—If I have anything, money, furniture, give to my mother Ruby Dandridge—She will know what to do.

THE actress Diahann Carroll still calls "the most beautiful black woman I've ever met in my life" was found lying on the bathroom floor, nude save for a blue scarf wrapped around her head. The woman who broke color barriers in Hollywood, the first African American to be nominated for an Academy Award for Best Actress (for *Carmen Jones*) was dead at forty-two. Soon afterward, the autopsy report was leaked, stating that Dandridge died from an embolism—a tiny fracture in her right foot sent bone marrow particles into her blood stream that reached her brain and lungs. Two months later, at a press conference in Los Angeles, the Los Angeles county chief medical examiner told reporters that the earlier analysis "was due to a lack of a complete study and pressure from news media," and that Dorothy had actually "died as a result of an overdose of drugs used to treat psychiatric depression."

Suicide? Accident? We still don't know. Her friend Diahann Carroll insists "Dorothy's desperation—having no work—led to her death." For a woman who had it all, she died leaving $4,000 worth of furniture and $2.14 in her bank account. On the outside of the envelope containing her suicide note, Dorothy had penned: "To Whomever Discovers Me After Death—Important."

GEORGE EASTMAN (1854–1932)
To my friends: My work is done. Why wait?

IN the final two years, the life of the founder of Eastman Kodak and the inventor of roll film was clearly not in focus. A degenerative disorder made it difficult for him to stand

and walk. He grew increasingly depressed. On March 14, the lifelong bachelor excused himself, went upstairs, had a cigarette, removed his glasses, and shot himself in the heart. A Kodak moment it was not.

His funeral was held at St. Paul's Episcopal Church in Rochester; only those employees who worked for the company for thirty years or more were allowed to view the body. In California, all movie-making was halted for one minute in honor of the man who invented film. He is buried on the grounds of Kodak Park in Rochester, New York.

ONA MUNSON (1906–1955)
This is the only way I know to be free again. Please don't follow me.

TALLULAH Bankhead turned down the role, saying it was "too small." So Munson accepted it, creating an indelible big-screen memory of voluptuous Belle Watling, the *Gone with the Wind* madam with a heart of gold and a head of red. Yet Munson's career never really took off the way it should have. Typecasting came too easily. At 1 p.m. on February 11, her husband found her dead in their New York City apartment. A fast gulp of lots of sleeping pills stilled the actress at fifty-one.

FREDDIE PRINZE (1954–1977)
I must end it. There's no hope left. I'll be at peace. No one had anything to do with this.
My decision totally.

IT began during the early morning hours of January 28, 1977, after Prinze received a restraining order from his ex-wife the previous evening. The comedian made a series of farewell phone calls to family, friends, and management from his hotel room at the Beverly Comstock Hotel. He told his mother, "Mom, I love you very much, but I can't go on. I need to find peace." He called his ex-wife and said, "I love you, Kathy. I love the baby, but I need to find peace. I can't go on." After the call, Prinze pulled out a gun from the sofa and shot himself in the head. He was rushed to the UCLA Medical Center and placed on life support following emergency surgery. Prinze's family pulled the plug, and the funny man died at 1 p.m. at the age of twenty-two. The death was ruled a suicide. His mother led the effort to have the cause of death reworded; years later Prinze's death was re-ruled an "accidental shooting due to the influence of Quaaludes."

GEORGE SANDERS (1906–1972)

Dear World: I am leaving you because I am bored. I feel I have lived long enough. I am leaving you with your worries in this sweet cesspool. Good luck.

THERE was never a doubt among those who knew him that the witty Englishman and former love slave to Zsa Zsa Gabor would kill himself. Fellow Brit thespian David Niven recalls that Sanders once told him, "I will have had enough of this earth by the time I am 65. After that, I shall be having my bottom wiped by nurses and suffer being pushed around in a wheelchair. I won't be able to enjoy a woman anymore, so I shall commit suicide." Which is exactly what he did on April 25. While on "vacation" in Barcelona in a rented seaside hotel room, he washed down five bottles of Nembutal with a bottle of vodka. He was, as promised, sixty-five.

JEAN SEBERG (1938–1979)

Diego, my dear son, forgive me. I can't live any longer with my nerves. I can't deal with a world that beats the weak, puts down the blacks and women and massacres infants. Understand me, I know that you can, and you know that I love you. You must be strong. Your mother who loves you, Jean.

ONCE upon a time, politics and Hollywood didn't mix. Remember Joe McCarthy or J. Edgar Hoover? In the late 1960s, critically acclaimed actress Seberg—plucked out of obscurity among eighteen thousand other hopefuls to star in the title role in Otto Preminger's 1957 epic *Saint Joan*—became increasingly active in left-wing political groups, especially in her support of the NAACP and Black Panthers. Nothing she did was illegal, but FBI-nervous Nelly Hoover watched her every move and tapped every phone. It was probably Hoover's henchmen who began the rumors that the father of the pregnant Seberg's child was not husband Romain Gary, but Raymond Hewt, a Black Panther leader. The actress was so sickened by the news that she gave birth, prematurely, to a daughter she named Nina, who died two days later. (Although Gary acknowledged Nina as his own, the father was actually a student revolutionary named Carlos Navarra with whom Seberg had a brief affair.) But Hoover wouldn't let up.

Seberg moved to Paris, divorced, fell into a deep depression, and became dependent on alcohol and prescription drugs; on every anniversary of Nina's death, she attempted suicide. On September 8, 1979, she was found in the backseat of her white Renault that was parked around the corner from her Paris apartment. A blue blanket covered her nude and decomposing body; she had been dead for ten days. (The guard who found her body was alarmed by the "strong smell" coming from the car.) The police report stated that Seberg had taken a massive overdose of barbiturates and alcohol. Her suicide note to her eighteen-year-old son was written in French, and English translations have always been as fuzzy as an alcohol-induced stupor. Questions abounded: How did Seberg manage to drive with that amount of alcohol in her body? And why were her driving glasses, which she insisted she needed for driving, left on her desk?

The answers were sucked away . . . by the power of a Hoover.

HUNTER S. THOMPSON (1937–2005)

Football Season Is Over.

No More Games. No More Bombs. No More Walking. No More Fun. No More Swimming. 67. That is 17 years past 50. 17 more than I needed or wanted. Boring. I am always bitchy. No Fun for anybody. 67. You are getting Greedy. Act your old age. Relax This won't hurt.

AUTHOR Tom Wolfe has lauded Thompson as "the century's greatest comic writer in the English language." Let's add witty. But we're getting ahead of ourselves. Thompson, in constant pain from myriad physical problems including a broken leg and hip replacement, shot himself in the head at his home in Woody Creek, Colorado, at 5:42 p.m. on February 20.The father of gonzo journalism went out with a bang of a .45. Two bangs actually. He was sitting at his typewriter, and only one word—*counselor*—was found on the blood-soaked piece of paper. Writer's block?

His will stipulated that his ashes be fired from a cannon atop a 153-foot tower of his own design—in the shape of a double-thumbed fist clutching a peyote button to the tune of Bob Dylan's "Mr. Tambourine Man." And so on August

20, pop went the ashes, along with red, blue, and green fireworks. Johnny Depp, a close chum of Hunter, paid for the final sendoff: "All I'm doing is trying to make sure his last wish comes true. I just want to send my pal out the way he wants to go out." Depp was one of about 280 people who attended the show; others in attendance included U.S. Senator John Kerry, former U.S. Senator George McGovern, *60 Minutes* correspondents Ed Bradley and Charlie Rose, Jack Nicholson, Bill Murray, Sean Penn, and Lyle Lovett. The suicide note was left for his wife, Anita, who, thanks to Hunter's impressive estate, never has to fear and loathe Las Vegas.

HERVÉ JEAN-PIERRE VILLECHAIZE (1943–1993)

I have to do what's right. At 6 years old I knew there was no place for me. Who believed my [illegible] best friend girl will not call my mom to answer the Q's. I hope she does not hurt. I'm still alive. Please know Kathy has the right of attorney over my health and my belongings belong to Kathy Self including the right to a script and movie and writings, etc. I love you all too much, it's one of just of my problems. Mom! My brothers you didn't exist to my heart you never care only about yourselves since 1955, you remember??? Kathy did her best, you didn't so she deserves everything.

3am I can't miss with a dum dum bullet—Ha! Ha! Never one knew my pain—for 40 years—or more. Have to do it outside less mess.

HERVÉ Villechaize gained fortune and instant recognition for his role as Tattoo ("De plane! De Plane!") in the hit TV series *Fantasy Island*. Then there was his juicy role as the evil Nick Nack in the 1974 James Bond flick *The Man with the Golden Gun*. So what went wrong, leading him to a write an (almost indiscernible) suicide note on a sheet of loose-leaf paper? The salary demands that the three-foot, ten-inch midget (he insisted that he not be referred to as a dwarf) made, along with his constant sexual harassment of females on the set and quarrels with the producers, got him fired. Suffering from ulcers, a spastic colon, and the effects of several strokes, the actor would sit in a darkened room, hurling obscenities at reruns of *Fantasy Island*. During the early morning hours of September 4, he disabled every phone in the house then shot himself in the backyard, using two pillows to muffle the sound as not to disturb his girlfriend Kathy Self, who accompanied him to a private screening of Harrison Ford's *The Fugitive* earlier that evening. He had a tape recorder with him; the tape (unlike the note) was clearer: "Kathy, I can't live like this anymore. I've always been a proud man and always wanted to make you proud of me. You know you made me feel like a giant and that's how I want you to remember me." After a bit more rambling he said, "I'm doing what I have to do. I want everything to go to Kathy. I want everyone to know that I love them."

JAMES WHALE (1889–1957)

The future is just old age and illness and pain. . . . I must have peace and this is the only way.

AS the director of such classic films as *Frankenstein*, *The Bride of Frankenstein*, and *The Invisible Man*, Whale kept us on the edge of our seats. Imagine how the movie man must have felt when, after suffering a stroke, he was left unable to draw or read or work on a new film. And so on Memorial Day, he shaved, showered, and penned the note. Then the nonswimmer went outside and dove headfirst in the shallow end of the pool. The dive only bruised his forehead . . . what killed Whale were the large amounts of water he purposely swallowed. Police made an additional macabre discovery: On Whale's nightstand was a book entitled *Don't Go Near the Water.*

WENDY O. WILLIAMS (1949–1998)

I don't believe that people should take their own lives without deep and thoughtful reflection over a considerable period of time. I do believe strongly, however, that the right to do so is one of the most fundamental rights that anyone in a free society should have. For me much of the world makes no sense, but my feelings about what I am doing ring loud and clear to an inner ear and a place where there is no self, only calm.

SHE went from making money selling crocheted string bikinis to working as a macrobiotic cook, a dancer with a gypsy dance troupe, and a performer in live sex shows. (Rent the porno film *Candy Goes to Hollywood*, famous for its "Ping-Pong ball scene" for Williams's other talent.) But Williams is best known as lead singer of the punk band the Plasmatics. With fame came notoriety—Williams quickly developed a reputation for obscenity and unruliness. Police arrested her in January of 1981 for simulating sex onstage; the group was once banned in London, where the press dubbed the Plasmatics "anarchists." Offstage, Williams was deeply devoted to the welfare of animals, working as a wildlife rehabilitator. So it remains a mystery why she decided to use a shotgun to kill herself in a wooded area near her home.

VIRGINIA WOOLF (1882–1941)

I feel certain that I am going mad again. I feel we can't go through another of those terrible times. And I shan't recover this time. I begin to hear voices, and I can't concentrate. So I am doing what seems the best thing to do. You have given me the greatest possible happiness. You have been in every way all that anyone could be. I don't think two people could have been happier till this terrible disease came. I can't fight any longer. I know that I am spoiling your life, that without me you could work. And you will I know. You see I can't even write this properly. I can't read. What I want to say is I owe all the happiness of my life to you. You have been entirely patient with me and incredibly good. I want to say that—everybody knows it. If anybody could have saved me it would have been you. Everything has gone from me but the certainty of your goodness. I can't go on spoiling your life any longer. I don't think two people could have been happier than we have been.

AFTER finishing the manuscript of her last (posthumously published) novel *Between the Acts*, Woolf became intimate with an old friend: depression. She was having another nervous breakdown, so she wrote a final note to her husband. Instead of popping pills or shooting herself, the old girl drowned herself by weighting her pockets with stones and walking into the freezing Ouse, a river in North Yorkshire, England. Her body was not found until April 18, nearly three weeks later.

Parting Is Such Sweet Sorrow

LAST BREATHS, LAST WORDS

HANS CHRISTIAN ANDERSEN (1805–1875)

Most of the people who will walk after me will be children, so make the beat keep time with little steps.

SUFFERING from liver cancer and bronchitis, the father of fairy tales died in the home of friends. He had been reading a "Dear John" letter, written forty-five years earlier by Riborg Voigt, the only woman he'd ever loved and who had rejected him. Hans kept the lengthy letter in a pocket pouch above his heart; the letter was destroyed when he was interred in the Assistens Kirkegård in Copenhagen.

MARIE ANTOINETTE (1755–1793)

Monsieur, I beg your pardon.

AND you thought Nancy Reagan was extravagant. The queen of France was considered arrogant and unashamed of her high-caloric lifestyle, suggesting that the poor should eat cake if they had no bread. Revolutionaries seized Paris in 1789, and Marie and her husband King Louis XVI were held prisoners until 1792 when they were charged with treason. Both were sentenced to die by beheading; Louis lost his on January 21, 1793. Marie followed him to her death in October of that same year, and did manage to apologize to the executioner when she stepped on his foot.

TALLULAH BANKHEAD (1902–1968)
Codeine, bourbon.

BANKHEAD, labeled "vibrant and tempestuous" by the *New York Times* in the headline of her obituary, knew few boundaries. She chain-smoked up to a hundred cigs a day, cussed up a storm, refused to wear underwear or close bathroom doors, and habitually abused alcohol (two bottles of Old Grand-Dad a day), opiates, and pot. She appeared on *The Lucy-Desi Comedy Hour* drunk, and once, when asked by a reporter if the rumor that Montgomery Clift was gay was true, she used her trademark wit and replied, "I have no idea, daaahling. He never sucked my cock!" Before the bisexual actress died from the Asian flu (she also had emphysema), she took one last look at the hospital ventilator and asked for two old-fashioned favorites. She was buried in a baby blue casket, dressed in a favorite silk dress (replete with cigarette burn marks) and holding a rabbit's foot.

P. T. BARNUM (1810–1891)
How were the receipts today at Madison Square Garden?

AMERICA'S greatest showman died in his sleep at his home and was buried in Mountain Grove Cemetery in Bridgeport,

Connecticut, a cemetery he designed himself. Just before his death, he gave permission to the *Evening Sun* to print his obituary, so that he might have a chance to read it. And so, on March 14, the headline read: GREAT AND ONLY BARNUM. HE WANTED TO READ HIS OBITUARY. HERE IT IS." Barnum died less than a month later, on April 7.

JOHN BARRYMORE (1882–1942)

Die? I should say not, dear fellow. No Barrymore would allow such a conventional thing to happen to him.

THE Great Profile collapsed while appearing on Rudy Vallee's radio show and died a few days later in his hospital room. Cause of death: cirrhosis of the liver and pneumonia. When W. C. Fields heard that his drinking buddy was on his deathbed, he sent him a telegram reading YOU CAN'T DO THIS TO ME. Film director Raoul Walsh "borrowed" Barrymore's body after the funeral (he bribed the undertaker with $200), and left his corpse propped in a chair for Errol Flynn to discover when he returned home from a night of drinking. Flynn recalled the morbid moment in his autobiography: "As I opened the door, I stared into the face of Barrymore. His eyes were closed. He looked puffed, white, bloodless. They hadn't embalmed him yet. I let out a delirious scream. My heart pounded. I couldn't sleep the rest of the night."

Barrymore left specific instructions that he be cremated and his ashes buried next to his parents in the family plot in Philadelphia. However, as brother Lionel Barrymore and sister Ethel Barrymore were Catholic and cremation was not sanctioned by the Church at the time, the executors of his estate had Barrymore's remains entombed at Calvary Cemetery in Los Angeles. In 1980, John Drew Barrymore decided to fulfill his father's wishes and have him cremated, and recruited his son to help. They had the casket removed from its Los Angeles crypt; before the body was cremated, John Jr. insisted on having a look inside. "Thank God I'm drunk," he told his son. "I'll never remember it."

Barrymore's ashes are interred in Mt. Vernon Cemetery in Philadelphia. His gravestone reminds one and all that the Great Profile was the greatest Hamlet of them all, with the line "Alas, Poor Yorick" engraved beneath his name.

HUMPHREY BOGART (1899–1957)
Hurry back.

RANKED by the American Film Institute as the greatest male star, Bogie had just turned fifty-seven and weighed only eighty pounds when he died, at 2:25 a.m. at his home in Holmby Hills, California, on January 14 of cancer of the esophagus. Wife Lauren Bacall—the last words were said to her as she left on a quick errand—asked Bogie's chum Spencer Tracy to give the eulogy, but he was too upset, so John Huston gave it instead. Buried with Bogie at Forest Lawn is a small gold whistle, which he had given to Bacall before they married. In reference to their first movie together, it was inscribed: "If you want anything, just whistle."

JOHN WILKES BOOTH (1838–1865)
Useless . . . useless.

THE man who killed Lincoln with a single gunshot to the back of his head (making Honest Abe the first American president to be assassinated) is more famous for his evil deed than his awful acting. After shooting the president Booth fled Ford's Theatre through the stage door, hopped on his waiting horse, and made his way to a northern Virginia farm where he hid in a tobacco shack. Soldiers tracked him down just before dawn on April 26. Booth refused to surrender, preferring "to come out and fight." The soldiers set the barn on fire; one shot the assassin while he was still inside the blazing building. Dragged outside, Booth died three hours later. The bullet pierced three vertebrae, severed his spinal cord and paralyzed him. Those listening closely heard him murmur, "Tell my mother I died for my country." Asking for help sitting up, he took a last look at his hands, and uttered his last words.

Booth's body was brought to the Washington Navy Yard, where friends identified him from the tattoo on his left hand with his initials J.W.B. and the scar on the back of his neck. (A diary, compass, candle, and pictures of his fiancée were found in Booth's pockets.) Two years after the body was buried in a storage room at the Old Penitentiary, the remains were given to the Booth family and were buried in the family plot in Green Mount Cemetery in Baltimore. (Though his exact grave remains unmarked, his name is on the reverse side of the main obelisk). Well, not all of him: His third, fourth, and fifth vertebrae were removed during the autopsy so investigators could access the bullet that killed him. Today, these relics are on display at Washington, DC's National Museum of Health and Medicine, not very far from Ford's Theatre.

JAMES BROWN (1933–2006)
I'm going away tonight.

THE hardest-working man in show business never knew when to quit. Two days before his death, Brown showed up (several hours late) at his dentist's office for some implant work. The dentist noticed that the Godfather of Soul looked "very bad . . . weak and dazed," and sent him off to his doctor. Brown was admitted to Emory Crawford Long Hospital in Atlanta, Georgia, on December 24; he died on Christmas Day at 1:45 a.m. from congestive heart failure resulting from complications of pneumonia. President Bush praised him as "an American original," while Rolling Stone Mick Jagger dubbed him a "one-of-a-kind, never-to-be-repeated star."

TRUMAN CAPOTE (1924–1984)

I'm cold.

THE author wasn't killed in cold blood but in that good old-fashioned way: an overdose. Tru took a handful of pills and was found dead in bed, without the chance for one last breakfast at Tiffany's, at the Bel-Air home of his longtime good pal Joanne Carson, the former wife of talk show host Johnny. (The official autopsy report stated death was from "liver disease complicated by phlebitis and multiple drug intoxication.") Capote was cremated, and his cremains were split between his long-term companion Jack Dunphy and Carson, who kept her share in a small urn in her home.

Then a scene that might as well have come straight from Capote's mind: Carson claims that during a 1988 Halloween party, someone stole the urn, along with sundry Capote memorabilia and $200,000 worth of her jewelry. Six nights later, she says a car screeched up to her house; when she went to investigate, Carson found that the thief had returned the ashes, leaving them inside a coiled garden hose on her back steps. That's when she decided to bury her portion of the cremains in Westwood Memorial Park. "I had to give him up to protect him," she said at the time. Besides the urn, Carson placed a letter she wrote inside the crypt that read, in part: "Tru love, wait for me.

I'll be joining you in time and we'll sail kites against the blue sky . . ."

It's a great story—and some insist it's just that, a story. According to Gerald Clarke, the executor of Capote's estate, Carson had/has some of Tru's ashes; the rest are "in a closed brass box that looks like a book and that is extremely heavy. They were on a shelf in Jack's apartment for all those years and now I have them." Well not all of them: When Dunphy died in 1992; some of his ashes were mixed with some of Tru's and scattered on Long Island. Dunphy's brother has the rest.

LEWIS CARROLL (1832–1898)
Take away the pillows.

THE author of *Alice in Wonderland* didn't fall down the rabbit hole, but he died at his sister's home, at 2:30 p.m. on January 14 of pneumonia contracted after a bout of following influenza. One of the funeral wreaths found at his grave was simply signed "Alice."

MONTGOMERY CLIFT (1920–1966)
Absolutely not!

AT about 1 a.m., when Clift's live-in personal secretary noticed that the actor's last film, *The Misfits*, was airing on TV, he knocked on his bedroom door to ask if he wanted to watch the movie. Perhaps Clift didn't want to be reminded that the 1961 film was the last screen appearance of his costars Clark Gable and Marilyn Monroe. Five hours later, Clift's lifeless nude body was discovered on his back in bed, with glasses on, right arm flexed, and fists clenched. Rigor mortis had set in. The cause of death: a heart attack brought on by occlusive coronary artery disease. One person noticeably absent from his funeral service was Elizabeth Taylor, who in 1956, after the actor had a major car crash, saved his life by removing two teeth that had become lodged in his throat. She was in Paris and sent flowers. Actress Nancy Walker, a good friend of the actor's, later planted two hundred crocuses on his grave in Friends Cemetery in Brooklyn.

LOU COSTELLO (1906–1959)

That was the best ice-cream soda I ever tasted.

HE was the chubby, cherubic half of Abbott and Costello, the comedy team whose roles as bumbling servicemen in *In the Navy* and *Keep 'Em Flying* were funny—and to some authentic: The Japanese government, believing Americans were so inept at war, screened the films for Japanese soldiers. Bud and Lou broke up in July 1957, after IRS troubles forced them to sell homes and the rights to some of their films. After making one solo film, *The 30 Foot Bride of Candy Rock*, Costello died of a heart attack on March 3, but not before sucking down the strawberry ice-cream soda he asked his agent to fetch him.

JOAN CRAWFORD (1905–1977)

Damn it! Don't you dare ask God to help me!

FRIENDS knew the end was near when Crawford gave away her beloved shih tzu Princess Lotus Blossom. She died two days later at her New York apartment from a heart attack; she was also suffering from breast and pancreatic cancer. Her last words were directed to her housekeeper, who had begun to pray out loud. A funeral was held at the Frank E.

Campbell funeral home on May 10, 1977. The woman who, during the filming of *Night Gallery*, taught director Steven Spielberg to burp, bequeathed to her two youngest children, Cindy and Cathy, $77,500 each from her $2,000,000 estate. However, she explicitly disinherited the two eldest, Christina and Christopher. In the last paragraph of the will, she wrote, "It is my intention to make no provision herein for my son Christopher or my daughter Christina for reasons which are well known to them." Crawford was cremated and her ashes placed in a crypt with her last husband, Pepsi chairman Alfred Steele, in Ferncliff Cemetery, Hartsdale, New York. Her birth year was changed to 1908 . . . to make her younger.

BING CROSBY (1903–1977)

That was a great game of golf, fellas. Let's go get a Coke.

HE sang, he danced, he acted, and he loved to play golf. Shortly after 6 p.m. on October 14, Crosby collapsed just twenty yards from the clubhouse, dying suddenly from a massive heart attack. He had just completed a round of eighteen holes near Madrid, where he and his Spanish golfing partner had just defeated their two opponents. (He scored an 85.) He's interred in the Holy Cross Cemetery in Culver City, next to his first wife. He was buried nine feet deep so that his second wife could be buried with him.

CANDY DARLING (1944–1974)

By the time you read this I will be gone. Unfortunately before my death I had no desire left for life . . . I am just so bored by everything. You might say bored to death. Did you know I couldn't last. I always knew it. I wish I could meet you all again.

ONE of the most famous pre-op transsexual stars to come out of Andy Warhol's Factory was only twenty-nine when she died from leukemia that developed as a result of the hormones she had been taking. She wrote these words on her deathbed, a final message to Andy and pals. The *New York Times* honored her by placing her obituary on the front page.

LEONARDO DA VINCI (1452–1519)
I have offended God and mankind because my work did not reach the quality it should have.

IT'S said that King François I held Leonardo's head in his arms as he died, although this story, beloved by the French and portrayed in many romantic paintings, is most likely an urban legend. We do know Leonardo sent for a priest to make his confession and to receive the holy sacrament. In accordance to his will, sixty beggars followed his casket, and he was buried in the Chapel of Saint-Hubert in the Castle of Amboise. His friend and apprentice, Count Francesco Melzi, was the principal heir and executor, receiving money, as well as Leonardo's paintings, tools, library, and personal effects. Leonardo also remembered another longtime pupil and companion and his servant, each of whom received half of Leonardo's vineyards. His maid received a black cloak with a fur edge.

JAMES DEAN (1931–1955)
That guy's gotta stop. He'll see us.

YEAH, right. On September 30, Dean and his mechanic took off in the actor's custom-made Porsche Spyder 550 headed for a car race at Salinas, California. At 3:30 p.m., Dean was ticketed in Kern County for doing sixty-five miles per hour in a fifty-five miles per hour zone. After stopping at Blackwell's Corner in Lost Hills for fuel, Dean was driving west on U.S. Route 466 near Cholame, California, when a black and white 1950 Ford Custom Tudor coupe, driven from the opposite direction by twenty-three-year-old Cal Poly student Donald Turnupseed, attempted to take the fork onto State Route 41. The late-afternoon sun blinded him, and he crossed into Dean's lane without seeing him; the two cars hit almost head-on. A heavily breathing Dean, almost decapitated in the crash, was placed into an ambulance and taken to Paso Robles War Memorial Hospital, where he was pronounced dead on arrival at 5:59 p.m. Turnupseed received a gashed forehead and bruised nose and was not cited by police for the accident. "I didn't see them, I swear I didn't," he moaned again and again.

The day before Dean's death, Hollywood writer James Bacon recalls seeing the actor doing eighty miles an hour on a Los Angeles street before screeching to a halt. As the actor got out of his Porsche Spyder, Bacon said, "Jimmy, that's a good way to keep from growing old." Dean shot back, "Who wants to grow old?"

Perhaps even more ironic: During the filming of *Giant*, Dean filmed a short promotional interview with actor Gig Young about the dangers of speeding. "The lives you might save might be mine," he ad-libbed. The footage, part of a Warner Brothers shorts series, never aired, but is one of the more popular YouTube destinations.

CECIL B. DEMILLE (1881–1959)

The Lord giveth and the Lord taketh away. Blessed be the Lord. It can only be a short time until these words are spoken over me.

THESE words were not spoken but written by the Oscar-winning film director just hours before he succumbed to heart failure. He knew the end was near when, while filming the Exodus scene for 1956's *Ten Commandments*, he climbed a 107-foot ladder and suffered a near fatal heart attack. Against his doctor's orders, he was back at work within a week. And dead shortly thereafter.

DIANA, PRINCESS OF WALES (1961–1997)
My God. What's happened?

FRANKLY, Diana, we don't know. The People's Princess, along with her lover Dodi Al-Fayed, was killed during a high-speed car crash in the Pont de l'Alma road tunnel in Paris. Henri Paul, the acting security manager of the Hotel Ritz Paris, whose blood analysis would later prove he was legally intoxicated, was driving the black 1994 Mercedes-Benz S280, eluding the paparazzi. He was also killed. The car crashed into the thirteenth pillar of the tunnel. None of the occupants were wearing seat belts. Dodi's bodyguard, Trevor Rees-Jones was the lone survivor. Diana, who was in the backseat, was violently thrown around the interior upon impact, "submarined" under the seat in front and suffering massive damage to her heart. The internal bleeding was a royal mess.

After a short delay, an ambulance whisked her to a hospital, where she went into cardiac arrest twice. Despite lengthy resuscitation attempts, including internal cardiac massage, she died at 4 a.m. She was buried dressed in a black long-sleeved dress designed by Catherine Walker. Rosary beads she received from Mother Teresa (who would die the same week) were placed in her hands, and photographs of her beloved sons William and Harry and her father were tucked into her oak coffin. Her funeral, held on September 6, was watched by an estimated 2.5 billion people worldwide and broadcast to 180 countries, the largest audience in TV history.

NELSON EDDY (1901–1967)

I can't see! I can't hear!

THE other half of the Jeanette MacDonald singing team was performing at the Sans Souci Hotel in Palm Beach, Florida, when he was stricken with a cerebral hemorrhage. He died a few hours later, in the early hours of March 6.

BOB FOSSE (1927–1987)

Please stop. You're hurting me. I'm all right. Don't worry about me.

ON September 23, the chain-smoking Tony- and Oscar-winning dance legend, working on a revival of his 1969 hit musical *Sweet Charity*, was walking back to his Washington, DC, hotel room. With him was former wife and original *Charity* star Gwen Verdon (they separated in the 1970s, but remained married); at about 7 p.m. when they reached the corner of 13th and Pennsylvania Avenue, Fosse fell to the ground, the victim of a massive heart attack. Gwen cradled his head in her arms and tried to shoo away the crowds that had gathered. A doctor worked his way through, loosened Fosse's shirt, and began pounding his heart. It obviously hurt, and Fosse, his eyes now half shut and his complexion green, said so. Fosse was rushed to the hospital, but nothing could save him. He died, at sixty, as opening night audience members at the Kennedy Center were enjoying the intermission of *Sweet Charity*. Verdon later told the press Fosse suffered the fatal heart attack and died in his room at the Willard, wanting to preserve his dignity. Papers fell for it, even the *New York Times*. Fosse's ashes were scattered at sea . . . and all that jazz.

STEPHEN FOSTER (1826–1864)

I'm done for.

THIS beautiful dreamer, the Father of American Music, was the preeminent songwriter of the nineteenth century. He died in poverty, in New York's Bellevue Hospital, three days after falling in his Bowery bathroom and severely cutting his throat on the broken basin. A friend finally found his alcohol-ravaged body at the local morgue; Foster's purse contained thirty-eight cents and a scrap of paper on which the words "dear friends and gentle hearts" were written . . . possibly the opening line to a new song.

BENJAMIN FRANKLIN (1706–1790)

A dying man can do nothing easy.

THE man whose face adorns the $100 bill, one of the Founding Fathers of America, died at eighty-four after an abscess in his lung burst and sent him into a coma. But his wish to prolong life has been frozen in time. In April 1773, he penned a letter to fellow scientist Jacques Dubourg, expressing this desire. In part, the missive read: "Your observations on the causes of death, and the experiments which you propose for recalling to life those who appear to be killed by lightning, demonstrate equally your sagacity and your humanity. It appears that the doctrine of life and death in general is yet but little understood . . . I wish it were possible . . . to invent a method of embalming drowned persons, in such a manner that they might be recalled to life at any period, however distant . . ."

Franklin's funeral was attended by approximately twenty thousand people, and he was interred in Christ Church Burial Ground in Philadelphia. In 1728, as a young man, he wrote what he hoped would be his own epitaph:

The Body of B. Franklin Printer; Like the Cover of an old Book, Its Contents torn out, And stript of its Lettering and Gilding, Lies here, Food for Worms. But the Work shall not be wholly lost: For it will, as he believ'd, appear once more, In a new & more perfect Edition, Corrected and Amended By the Author.

Franklin's actual grave, however, as he specified in his final will, simply reads, Benjamin and Deborah Franklin: 1790.

JAMES D. FRENCH (1936–1966)
How's this for a headline? "French Fries."

ONCE French was found guilty of murder, he tried to appeal his sentence by insisting his constitutional rights were "violated" since he had to attend his trial "clothed in the tell-tale prison garb and surrounded by prison guards." He claimed that such actions could "only be construed as forcing himself to give testimony to his alleged vile and dangerous character." Funny, the only prisoner executed in the United States in 1966 could have written jokes for a living . . . if the electric chair didn't fry him.

JOHN WAYNE GACY (1942–1994)

Kiss my ass!

THE Killer Clown—so named because he made a living entertaining kids as Pogo the Clown—was convicted of the rape and murder of thirty-two men, twenty-eight of whom he buried in a crawl space under the floor of his house and garage. He admitted dumping some bodies in the river when he ran out of room at home—plus, all the grave-digging was causing him back problems. Gacy would lure his victims into being handcuffed and then he would sexually assault them. To muffle the screams of his victims, he would stuff a sock or underwear into their mouths and kill them by pulling a rope or board against their throats as he raped them. Gacy admitted to sometimes keeping the dead bodies under his bed or in the attic for several hours before eventually disposing of them. His execution by lethal injection was supposed to take five minutes, but it took eighteen and Gacy struggled as the poison clogged his veins. Cruel and unusual punishment? Or God clowning around?

GARY MARK GILMORE (1940–1977)

Let's do it!

CONVICTED of killing a motel manager in Provo, Utah, Gilmore was put to death on January 17 by a volunteer firing squad. He was the first person legally executed in the United States since 1967, after a decade-long lapse in American executions. His request to have his death televised was tuned out.

EDMUND GWENN (1875–1959)
But it's harder to do comedy.

YES, Virginia, there is a Santa Claus. And his name is Edmund Gwenn, an English stage actor who won an Academy Award as the Best Supporting Actor in *Miracle on 34th Street* for his role as Kris Kringle. When he won the naked golden statuette, he exclaimed, "Now I know there is a Santa Claus!" He died of pneumonia, brought on by a stroke. But he was quick enough to offer a sassy retort when a friend, standing by the actor's deathbed, remarked that "it's hard to die." Gwenn was cremated but his remains are in a "storage vault" at the Chapel of the Pines Crematory in Los Angeles—the area is closed off to the public.

CONRAD NICHOLSON HILTON SR. (1887–1979)
Please leave the shower curtain on the inside of the tub.

IT'S no surprise that a man born on Christmas Day would give the world such a luxurious present: a chain of top-notch hotels that bear his name. (He is also the great-grandfather of Paris Hilton and Nicky Hilton, for which we forgive him.) On his deathbed, Hilton was asked if he had any words of wisdom. He pulled out a quote he once said on Johnny Carson's late-night show.

VICTOR HUGO (1802–1885)
I see black light.

FOR Hugo, there was nothing as middle ground when it came to the Roman Catholic Church. The writer and statesman viewed the Church as indifferent to the working class. So intense was his hatred, that when his sons Charles and François-Victor died, Hugo insisted that they be buried without a crucifix or the presence of a priest—he made the same stipulation about his own death and funeral. His death, at eighty-three, was cause for national mourning. His funeral procession through Paris from the Arc de Triomphe to his burial place in the Panthéon attracted nearly two million people.

KING GEORGE V (1865–1936)

God damn you!

HE was one royal mess: A heavy smoker, George suffered from bronchitis, emphysema, chronic obstructive lung disease, and pleurisy—he even needed oxygen now and then. On the evening of January 15, 1936, George, complaining of a cold, went to his room . . . and never came out alive. Five days later, as death was closing in faster, he mumbled his last words to a nurse after she administered a sedative. It wasn't just any sedative but a lethal injection of cocaine and morphine ordered by his doctor, who later admitted that he hastened the king's demise so that the royal obit could be announced in the morning edition of the *Times*. This is what's known as making a deadline.

GERTRUDE LAWRENCE (1898–1952)

See that Yul gets star billing. He has earned it.

THE English musical comedy star fainted after a Saturday matinee of *The King and I*, in which she was starring (and receiving top billing) as schoolteacher Anna Leonowens.

Doctors thought she was suffering from hepatitis, but her former son-in-law, a doctor at the hospital, suspected liver cancer. He was right. Lawrence's last performance took place three weeks before she died. More than five thousand people crowded the streets for Lawrence's funeral. She was buried in the champagne-colored gown she wore for the second act "Shall We Dance?" number in *The King and I* . . . and, yes, Yul got top billing.

WLADZIU VALENTINO LIBERACE (1919–1987)

It's beautiful in heaven, Mother. Yes of course I'll play the piano for you. I'll be with you soon and I'll play all the songs you love.

HIS friends called him Lee, his family called him Walter, and his boy toys called him rich. Onstage, his act was filled with gimmicks and garnish costumes; offstage his attention was lavished on loved ones and cars and dogs and very expensive homes. Yet the original piano man went to his grave denying he was dying from AIDS. When a reporter once asked him with whom he slept, Liberace quixotically answered, "Them." When the paparazzi caught the first glimpses of gaunt Liberace, his longtime manager and protector Seymour Heller attributed the weight loss to a watermelon diet. His manager worked overtime, confusing the public by planting stories that Liberace was romantically involved with women such as ice skater Sonja Henie, sex symbol Mae West, and transsexual Christine Jorgenson. Before he died, he lapsed in and out of comas, carrying on conversations with his (dead) mother, Gladys, (dead) brother, Rudy, and (dead) dog, Baby Boy. On the evening of February 3, 1987, Liberace lapsed into a final coma; those by his bedside—including Heller, his accountant, and his housekeeper, heard it all, including this deathbed diatribe directed at Mama: "I've kept it from the world, but you know my secret. Please forgive me Mom."

At 10:35 the next morning, Liberace, a rosary on his hand, fell into a final coma. His physician pronounced him dead at 2:05 p.m. A nurse placed his toupee on his head, combed the fake hair, washed the emaciated body, and tied a hospital gown around his corpse. A half hour later, Liberace's body was removed from his house by Forest Lawn employees, who wheeled him on a gurney in a black plastic body bag. Four hours after his embalming, the state rejected the death certificate and demanded an autopsy—under California law, one must be conducted if the person is suspected of or known to have a contagious disease. Tissue samples from the embalmed body were taken, and when the hospital refused to release Liberace's medical records, a court had them seized. The autopsy revealed that Liberace was HIV-positive. The mononymous musician was finally laid to rest in Forest Lawn Memorial Park in Los Angeles in an elaborate white marble tomb, also housing his mother and brother. A reproduction of Liberace's signature and a drawing of a piano adorn the front . . . along with the phrase "sheltered love."

VACHEL LINDSAY (1879–1931)
I got them before they could get me! They can just try and explain this if they can!

THE father of lyrical poetry took a less than poetic end to his life. A week after returning from a lecture tour, Lindsay, sickly and depressed over money matters, arranged photos of his wife and children in an orderly fashion in their Springfield, Illinois, home, lit two candles, and at one in the morning, drank a bottle of Lysol that he had poured into a glass . . . but not before he shouted his parting prose.

When she heard his cry, his wife rushed from the bedroom to find Lindsay dying on the floor. So shocking was the suicide that Lindsay's doctor said the cause of death was heart failure, a "fact" newspapers printed. The truth was finally revealed in 1935, when friend and fellow poet Edgar Lee Masters wrote a biography of Lindsay.

MALCOLM LITTLE (MALCOLM X, 1925–1965)
Let's cool it, brothers . . .

THEY didn't. On February 21, in Manhattan's Audubon Ballroom, the civil rights activist had just begun delivering a speech to a crowd of about four hundred when a disturbance broke out. As he and his bodyguards moved to quiet the crowd, a man rushed forward and shot Malcolm in the chest with a sawed-off shotgun. Two other men charged the stage and fired handguns at Malcolm, who was shot sixteen times. Onlookers caught and beat the assassins as they attempted to flee. Malcolm was pronounced dead on arrival at New York's Columbia Presbyterian Hospital. His body was on public viewing at Harlem's Unity Funeral Home for four days, and nearly thirty thousand people filed past his body. Malcolm X was buried at the Ferncliff Cemetery in Hartsdale; friends took shovels away from the waiting gravediggers and buried Malcolm themselves.

W. SOMERSET MAUGHAM (1874–1965)
Dying is a very dull, dreary affair. And my advice to you is to have nothing whatever to do with it.

ALTHOUGH he graduated in 1897 from medical school and qualified as a doctor, Maugham's prescription for success was writing—in fact, he was the highest-paid author in the world in the 1930s. Human bondage he cared for. Death he did not.

SAL MINEO (1939–1976)
Oh, no! Oh, my God! Help me, please!

EVERYONE knew Sal Mineo was gay, so when the former heartthrob was stabbed in the garage port of his rented West Hollywood apartment on February 12, people assumed it was a trick gone bad. At about 9 p.m., after Mineo had finished rehearsals of the gay-themed stage play *P.S. Your Cat Is Dead*, he got into his blue Chevelle and drove home. Sal parked the car and was walking to his door when he was attacked. Apartment complex tenant Ron Evans heard a man scream, ran outside, and saw Mineo bleeding. He turned the actor onto his back. Evans recalls that Sal's shirt was soaked with blood and he was having trouble breathing. As Evans gave Sal mouth-to-mouth resuscitation, someone called for an ambulance. Then Evans heard Mineo give a final exhale and he knew the final curtain had fallen; Mineo was pronounced dead at 9:55 p.m. A single stab that cut his heart killed him. Police found $21 in Sal's coat; the jewelry he was wearing and his car keys were lying next to his body, as was a copy of the play's script.

Mineo's autopsy found evidence of possible drug use; several puncture wounds were discovered in his buttocks and in other areas of his body. Everyone knew he used LSD, cocaine, and pot, but the puncture wounds suggested the use of heroin, though a former lover of the actor's explained the marks by admitting to police that Sal received hormone injections to supplement his waning sexual appetite. Some suggested the murder was drug-related; others insisted it was sex-related, especially after detectives found a huge stash of gay porno magazines in Sal's apartment. The body was flown back to New York for the funeral. On February 17, five days after Sal's murder, about 250 mourners crammed into Holy Trinity Roman Catholic Church in Mamaroneck, New York, including Hollywood chums Paul Newman, Natalie Wood, Warren Beatty, Desi Arnaz Jr., David Cassidy, Yul Brynner, Peter Lawford, and Dennis Hopper. A nineteen-year-old pizza deliveryman, Lionel Ray Williams, was charged with the crime after he bragged about it while he was incarcerated in a Michigan jail. He claimed he had no idea who Mineo was. Sentenced to fifty-seven years in prison, Williams was paroled in the early 1990s, but was soon jailed again for criminal activity.

SIR LAURENCE OLIVIER (1907–1989)

This isn't Hamlet, you know! It's not meant to go into the bloody ear!

LEAVE it to the actor many consider to be the greatest thespian of the twentieth century to go out with such an ad-libbed—and very funny—bit of dialogue. As Olivier lay in his bed, dying of a rare degenerative muscle disorder, a nurse leaned over to wet the parched lips of the eighty-two-year-old actor. She missed. He was cremated and his ashes interred in Poets' Corner in London's Westminster Abbey. Sharing some floor space with Olivier is noted thespian David Garrick (1716–1779), as famous in his days as Olivier was in his; legend had it that Garrick performed as Richard III with a bone fracture, inspiring the line "Break a leg!"

EUGENE O'NEILL (1888–1953)

I knew it. I knew it. Born in a hotel room and God damn it! Died in a hotel room.

HIS was a life of long days into nightmares. O'Neill suffered from multiple health problems, including alcoholism and a severe tremor that made it impossible for the playwright to write during his last decade. He died in Room 401 of the Sheraton Hotel in Boston on November 27. The building is now a Boston University dormitory that students insist he haunts. Though it was widely believed O'Neill had suffered from Parkinson's disease, he actually had cerebellar cortical atrophy, a neurological disease that usually affects horses and dogs.

EVA PERÓN (1919–1952)

Eva se va.

QUICK! How many South American sidewalk-strutting star-lets have been the subjects of a Tony-winning musical? Right, just the one. The life of Eva Perón was fraught with deceit and decay, but it was Evita's death that makes for the really scandalous stuff. When she died, the first lady of Argentina had been suffering from cervical cancer that had metastasized in her lungs. (Evita was the first Argentine to undergo chemotherapy.) She weighed just seventy-nine pounds at the time of her death; her last words, "Eva is leaving," were spoken to her sister. The news of her demise was immediately broadcast throughout the country, and Argentina went into mourning. Traffic was congested, eight people were trampled to death, and more than two thousand people hurt as throngs tried to get close to Evita as her body, soldered shut in a $30,000 bronze casket, was being taken from the Presidential Palace to the Ministry of Labour Building, where she would she lay in state.

Then the fun really started.

Plans were made to construct a monument in Evita's honor, her body to be "stored" in its base. For two years, while the monument was being built, Evita's body was displayed in her former office. The reason she looked so good all that time? Her corpse was drained of blood and replaced with glycerin, an ambitious embalming method that anatomy professor Dr. Pedro Ara assured would give his client "artistically rendered sleep."

When Evita's hubby Juan Perón was overthrown in a military coup in 1955, he fled the country, leaving Evita behind. For sixteen years, no one knew what happened to Evita's body. One day—perhaps out of guilt?—military officials finally revealed what they had done with the corpse—they had buried Evita in a crypt in Milan, Italy, under the name "Maria Maggi." In 1971, her body was exhumed and flown to Spain, where Juan kept the corpse in his home. Two years later, he returned to Argentina, becoming president for the third time. His wife at the time, Isabel Perón, had Evita's body returned to Argentina and buried in the family tomb in La Recoleta Cemetery in Buenos Aires. Could Evita disappear again? Hardly. She's hidden under a series of secret trapdoors and compartments. Reports claim the grave is so secure it could withstand a nuclear attack.

ELVIS PRESLEY (1935–1977)

I'm going into the bathroom to read.

WE assume he was looking for some new recipes? By the time Elvis died he weighed in at more than three hundred pounds. On August 16, the day before he was headed out for a concert, Presley's fiancée, Ginger Alden, found him on the bathroom floor of Graceland at about 2:30 in the afternoon. He had been there for nearly three hours, lying in a pool of his own vomit. Presley had been using the toilet at the time; his pajama bottoms had fallen to his ankles. He was pronounced dead at 3:30 p.m. at Baptist Memorial Hospital. An autopsy found fourteen different drugs in Presley's bloodstream, as well as toxic levels of methoqualone and ten times the normal dosage of codeine. The singer allegedly spent at least $1 million annually during his later years on drugs and doctors' fees. But for the record, his death was attributed to "cardiac arrhythmia" brought on by "undetermined causes." Hey, don't clogged arteries get any credit?

His funeral turned into a media circus; hundreds of thousands of fans lined the streets hoping to have a chance to see the open casket. (Two days after the singer's death, a car plowed into a group of more than two thousand fans outside Graceland, killing two women and critically injuring a third.) He was buried wearing a white suit and tie and a blue shirt his dad had given him for Christmas; on a finger was the famous TCB ring—always Taking Care of Business, this guy. Daughter Lisa Marie, then just nine years old, asked the funeral director to place a thin metal bracelet on her dad's right wrist; former wife Priscilla asked that the bracelet be covered by his sleeve so that no one would steal it as a souvenir. The casket was made from nine hundred pounds of seamless copper and was covered with roses; it cost $8,000 and was identical to the one in which his mother, Gladys, was buried when she died in 1980. Also buried with the King: a two-by-four-inch stainless steel cylinder for identification purposes in the event he is ever exhumed. A chemically treated piece of paper lists his full name, birth and death dates, as well as dates and places of his eulogy and burial. The crypt was sealed with two slabs of concrete and one slab of marble. Suspicious minds who want to know how the National Enquirer managed to nab a photo of Presley in his coffin that ended up on the tabloid's front cover: Presley cousin Bobby Mann secretly photographed the body and was paid $18,000. We still think we last saw Elvis at the Buttocks, Montana, Burger King having it his way.

GRIGORI YEFIMOVICH RASPUTIN (1869–1916)
You bad boy!

SIZE *does* matter. Floating in formaldehyde in a huge glass jar at the Museum of Erotica in St. Petersburg, Russia, is an awesome hunk o' flesh: the eleven-inch penis of the Mad Monk . . . and we're not including shrinkage caused by pickling. (No wonder he wore a loose-fitting cassock.) The museum's director bought the "object," along with several of Rasputin's hand-written letters, from a French antique dealer for $8,000. We assume it came with a certificate of authenticity.

Despite his reputation for faith healing and debauched behavior, Rasputin rose to preeminence within government circles. He was considered influential and intoxicating—he had a close relationship with Tsar Nicholas II's wife, Empress Alexandra. The heir to the throne suffered from hemophilia, and the royal family believed only Rasputin could stop the boy's bleeding. Alexandra and other noble women were so intoxicated by the bearded man (and his member) that they reportedly "worshipped" with him—a litany that was rumored to involve Christianity and regular relations of the sexual kind.

And then the tide turned. By the end of 1916, an army of aristocrats, led by Prince Felix Yussupov, decided that Rasputin's pervasive influence over the imperial family had grown too great, and that there was only one way to save Russia . . . by killing Rasputin. Here's where things get as muddled as Monday in Moscow. Legend claims that on December 29, Rasputin was lured to the prince's palace, fed sweet cakes and red wine laced with cyanide, shot four times, and severely beaten . . . and did not die. It was then that Rasputin uttered his last words to Yussupov, who in an act of desperation, wrapped him in a sheet (some say carpet) and threw him, still alive, into the icy waters of Russia's Neva River. When his body was pulled from the water, police found Rasputin's hands frozen in a raised position—making everyone believe that he had still been alive while submerged and had tried to untie the rope around his hands.

Back to the penis. According to those in the know, his manhood was separated by the murdering nobles. A maid found the penis at the crime scene and saved it, giving it in the 1920s to a group of Russian women living in Paris who worshipped the ample appendage as a holy relic/fertility charm. (They kept it inside a mini wooden casket.) When Rasputin's daughter, Marie, got wind of the whereabouts of her papa's penis, she demanded it back and it stayed safely (and presumably preserved) with her until she died in California in 1977.

Now you can believe two things: The thing on display at the Museum of Erotica is indeed Rasputin's organ, or this is merely a cock and bull story, and that "organ" is merely an oversize sea cucumber.

Rasputin was buried on the grounds of Tsarskoye Selo, the lavish estate given by Peter the Great to his wife, future Empress Catherine I—but Alexander Kerensky, the head of the Russian provisional government, demanded his body be moved to a remote cemetery. A group of revolutionaries uncovered the remains and burnt them in the woods. Here's where it gets even spookier: As the body was being consumed by flames, Rasputin "sat" up in the fire. A true miracle man? No, just bad cremation. Rasputin's tendons were not cut prior to cremation, so when his body heated up, they shrank, causing his legs and body to bend at the waist.

JOHN ARTHUR SPENKELINK (1949–1979)
Capital punishment—them without the capital get the pun-ishment.

THE drifter was convicted of killing a traveling companion, an act he swore was self-defense. Spenkelink was the first man put to be put to death in Florida after the Supreme Court reinstated capital punishment in 1976. A masked man flipped a red switch, sending 2,250 volts of electricity through John's wiry body, then an extra two surges. A doctor pronounced him dead at 10:18 a.m. But rumors about his death did not die quietly. After the execution, speculation spread that the gagged Spenkelink was already dead before the juice surged through his body; that he had been dragged to the chair, and that he was beaten and his neck broken. His body was exhumed—the rumors were just that—but from then on, the State of Florida decided to perform autopsies on all executed inmates. In a twist of fate, later that spring, convicted serial killer Ted Bundy would occupy the same cell at Florida State Prison.

SHARON TATE (1943–1969)
Mother, mother . . .

ON August 9, when police were summoned to the Benedict Canyon house Roman Polanski rented for his wife, the eight-months' pregnant actress had already been stabbed to death. The woman who got her first big break as a secretary on an episode of *The Beverly Hillbillies*, helped *Valley of the Dolls* become a camp classic, measured in at 36-22-35, and kept jars of her favorite lip makeup, Vaseline, in her car, was gone. Besides Tate and her unborn son, the carnage included hairstylist friend Jay Sebring (1933–1969), mountain-grown coffee heiress Abigail Folger (1943–1969), her boyfriend Wojciech Frykowski (1936–1969), and Steven Parent (1951–1969), who was leaving the property after visiting his friend, caretaker William Garretson.

For a town that is rarely shocked, Hollywood was terrorized. The infamous Manson Family had paid a visit to 10050 Cielo Drive. Fanatic Charles Manson was the leader of "the Family," a group of followers who believed what he preached and prophesied: that a race war was inevitable, and that blacks would triumph against whites and wipe them out. Manson preached to his "Family" that they would hide in a hole in the desert until the Black and White Holocaust was over, then they would have dominion over the world, with Manson emerging as Jesus Christ, ruling as one of five co-prophets—the other four prophets being the Beatles!

Scary stuff. What's scarier is that the unemployed ex-con didn't actually commit the carnage. He instructed his followers to "totally destroy everyone . . . as gruesome as you can"; he (and his "family members") received life in prison for masterminding these murders and the murder of a husband and wife two days later. In a jailhouse confession, Manson member Susan Atkins—who was promised immunity from prosecution—claimed that it was she who actually stabbed Tate to death. Restraining Tate while her friends were brutally butchered before her eyes, Atkins said she coldly told the terrified actress that she would be murdered and that there was nothing she could do about it. As Atkins repeatedly stabbed Tate, the dying actress cried out in anguish for her own mother. Atkins confessed that she then tasted Tate's blood, and used a towel dipped in Tate's blood to write DEATH TO PIGS on the wall and PIG on the front door. Tate and her unborn baby boy, named Paul Richard Polanski, were buried in Holy Cross Cemetery, Culver City, California. Manson, Corcoran State Prison inmate No. B33920, has been denied parole eleven times. He will be eligible again in 2012.

DYLAN THOMAS (1914–1953)
I've had eighteen straight whiskies, I think that's the record . . .

IT was November 5, and Dylan was starting to feel sick. He had been guzzling booze at New York City's White Horse Tavern, then staggered back to his room at the Hotel Chelsea, where he collapsed and slipped into a coma. An ambulance took him to St. Vincent's Hospital where he died four days later at about 1 p.m. "Chronic alcohol poisoning" was eventually ruled as the official cause of death; his liver, according to the pathologist, was amazingly healthier than one would have imagined.

VINCENT VAN GOGH (1853–1890)
The sadness will never go away.

FIRST it was his ear. Then his ribs. Disgusted with life and suffering from insanity, the Dutch Impressionist went into the wheat fields on a hot July day and shot himself in the chest. He was aiming for his heart, but one of his ribs deflected the bullet. The painter spent two days in agony, smoking his pipe when not curled up in bed. The day before he died, he uttered these words to his brother Theo.

OSCAR WILDE (1854–1900)
Either that wallpaper goes or I do.

HE with the sharp Irish wit and homosexual tendencies died of cerebral meningitis. Opinions differ as to the cause of the disease: Some say it was syphilitic; others claim the meningitis followed a surgical intervention, perhaps a mastoidectomy. Wilde's physicians reported that the condition stemmed from an old suppuration of the right ear. On his deathbed, Wilde was received into the Roman Catholic Church and Father Cuthbert Dunne administered baptism and extreme unction. Wilde was buried in the Cimetière de Bagneux outside Paris but was later moved to Père Lachaise Cemetery in Paris. His tomb in Père Lachaise was designed by sculptor Sir Jacob Epstein, at the request of Robert Ross, Wilde's first lover, who also asked for a small compartment to be made for his own ashes. Ross's ashes were transferred to the tomb in 1950. Visit the grave and you'll find numerous lipstick traces from admirers. Perhaps most telling is that the sculpture's penis was broken off decades ago and never replaced.

FLORENZ ZIEGFELD (1869–1932)

Curtain! Fast music! Lights! Ready for the last finale! Great! The show looks good. The show looks good.

EVEN as the final curtain was about to drop, the theater's greatest showman—as famous for his beautiful women as his shows' elaborate sets—knew just what to say . . . even if he was hallucinating at Burkeley Crest, his Hastings-on-the-Hudson estate. His wife, the actress Billie "Glinda the Good Witch" Burke, reached his bedside two minutes after he died. The Glorifier of the American Girl was in his final glory.

ACKNOWLEDGMENTS

MY name is on the cover of this book, but I did not write it myself. I've had lots of help and guidance from people who are dead. Though I have disinterred and dissected their deaths piece by piece, I am certain they continue to rest in peace . . . even the mean ones.

I thank all of them, and still wish I could have met Darnell and Dillinger.

Throughout the years, I *have* met countless people we have come to call "celebrities." Just about all of them have given me insight into their thoughts about the afterlife, reincarnation, death, and dying. I've used some of that info here. I cannot thank them all, but a selected few must be spotlighted: Lucie Arnaz, Kaye Ballard, Rona Barrett, Jim Belushi, Helen Gurley Brown, Richard Carpenter, Diahann Carroll, Cher, Joan Collins, Doris Day, Bob Eubanks, Michael J. Fox, Eydie Gorme, Mariska Hargitay, Julie Harris, Florence Henderson, Dennis Hopper, Steve Lawrence, Lorna Luft, Reba McEntire, Liza Minnelli, Jennifer O'Neill, Betsy Palmer, Dolly Parton, Suzanne Somers, Robert Wagner, and Stephanie Zimbalist.

The biggest thankful hug goes to Joan Rivers, who I've

known for thirty years, and who jump-started this project. In 2008 I was whining to her and she cut me off: "You're alive. You have friends. You love what you do. Shut up and get off your ass." I love her, too.

In California, a handful of people guided me along, some without knowing it: Jean-Noel Bassior, Ken Bird, Bruce Fessier and Jamie Lee Pricer of the Palm Springs *Desert Sun*, Andy Hamling, Don Martin, Roger Orlando, Karen Storey, Donna Theodore, Rev. Bill Thompson, and Betty Wilton. Mark Graves (great name!) of the Palm Springs Desert Resorts first introduced me to the pleasures of dead desert denizens. Dr. Rory Goshorn deserves to be called a "lifesaver," and I mean that literally. Clichés be damned, but words cannot express what he has done. I am forever grateful.

Those who offered moral and/or spiritual support: Caitlin Cahill, Kenneth G. Danchik, Greer Reed-Jones, Kathy Mahoney, Michael Musto, Dr. Lisa Pawelski, Jocelyn Pickett, Robert Osbome and Sarah Schmitz of Turner Classic Movies, Susan Sparks, and Bob Weis have been greatly supportive, and Paul Leroy Gehres is the only person I know who will join me for hours in the bitter cold looking for a famous grave—in this case, Elizabeth Hartman. We finally found her.

John Anthony Gilvey, author of *Before the Parade Passes By*, helped me track down Gower Champion's actual birth year. Garry McGee, author of *Jean Seberg—Breathless*, killed lots of Seberg urban legends so I could print the truth. Dr. John Carter Brooks, Earl Grey, and Debbie Szajna have kept me (in)sane. Ken Herbst helped me get ahead with Jayne Mansfield's tragic ending. Susan Schonfeld of Celestis Inc. was my *Star Trek* tour guide. Rick Armstrong and Ben Harrison of the Andy Warhol Museum, Mary Lu Denny of Pittsburgh History and Landmarks Foundation, Richard Engel of Pittsburgh Filmmakers, Michael K. Mackin of the

Heinz History Center and Bill McDonald, the *New York Times* obituary editor, allowed me to pick their brains . . . again and again. The staff of the Oakland branch of the Carnegie Library of Pittsburgh has my—do I dare?—undying gratitude.

A special nod must be given to former *Pittsburgh Post-Gazette* assistant managing editor Steve Massey for embracing the new kid in town.

Bob Hoover led me to Folio Literary Management and my agent, Erin C. Niumata—a hip, cool, smart agent who knows when to push . . . and when not to. Jeanette Shaw edited the manuscript with a keen eye, polishing it until it gleamed as brightly as, well, a marble gravestone. Megan Swartz and the rest of the Penguin publicity team will, I hope, make me rich.

Susan L. Glover and Kimberly Reynolds of the Boston Public Library hauled out the death masks and ashes of Sacco and Vanzetti on short notice that frigid January morning.

Edward F. Maroney, Rob and Toni Sennott, and David Still II, always the backbone of the *Barnstable Patriot*, have been friends and confidants for more years than I can remember. They allow me to rant and review on their pages.

Anita Fore of the Author's Guild answered every email and call. Quickly.

Steve Bennett of AuthorBytes.com created a website (www.deadcelebsbook.com) to die for!

And as always, then, now, and forever, undying love to Kevin M. Boyle, RN (1957–1998). *Requiescat in pace.*

INDEX